THE RISE OF AN INDUSTRIAL GIANT

The Rise of an Industrial Giant

THE STORY OF
AMERICA

THE RISE OF AN INDUSTRIAL GIANT

Editor in Chief
Henry Steele Commager

Editors
Marcus Cunliffe
Maldwyn A. Jones
Edward Horton

TORSTAR BOOKS
New York · Toronto

EDITOR IN CHIEF: Henry Steele Commager, now Professor
Emeritus at Amherst College, has taught at Columbia,
Cambridge, Oxford and other universities. In a long and
illustrious career he has written many books in his own
right, including *Theodore Parker, The American Mind,
Majority Rule and Minority Rights*, and *The Empire of
Reason*. He is the co-author (with Samuel Eliot Morison) of
The Growth of the American Republic, editor of *Documents
of American History*, and (with Richard B. Morris) of the
fifty-volume *New American Nation* series.

SENIOR EDITORS: Marcus Cunliffe, now University Professor
at George Washington University, and formerly of
Manchester and Sussex Universities, has also taught at
Harvard and Michigan. His books include *The Literature of
the United States, George Washington: Man and
Monument, Soldier and Civilians, The American
Presidency*, and *Chattel Slavery and Wage Slavery*.
Maldwyn A. Jones is Commonwealth Fund Professor of
American History at the University of London. He has been
a visiting professor at Harvard and at the Universities of
Chicago and Pennsylvania. He has written extensively on
American ethnic groups. His books include *American
Immigration*, a volume in the *Chicago History of American
Civilization*, and *The Limits of Liberty: American History,
1607-1980*.

TORSTAR BOOKS INC
41 Madison Avenue, Suite 2900
New York, NY 10010

Contributors to this volume include: Marcus Cunliffe, George
Washington University; Lewis L. Gould, University of Texas at Austin;
Rhodri Jeffreys-Jones, University of Edinburgh; Maldwyn A. Jones,
University of London; Blake McKelvey, City Historian of Rochester,
New York; John G. Sproat, University of South Carolina; Melvyn B.
Stokes, University College, London; Barry Supple, St. Catharine's
College, Cambridge.

ISBN 1-55001-063-8 (The Story of America Series)
ISBN 1-55001-083-2 (The Rise of an Industrial Giant)
The Story of America is also published as
The American Destiny
© 1975 Grolier Enterprises Inc
Printed in Yugoslavia

Introduction

In the last third of the nineteenth century American life moved to a new tempo. Rapid industrial growth was the keynote. While American industry had been developing steadily since the 1820s, it now experienced an astonishing upsurge. In Britain the Industrial Revolution had spanned a century; in America it occupied only a third of that time. Within a single generation Americans moved out of the horse-and-buggy age into the age of electricity and steel. By 1900, the United States had become the world's leading industrial power. Every aspect of national life was transformed by the economic revolution. The characteristic features of modern America now took shape: the vast, mushrooming city, machinery and mass production, the mammoth corporation.

Providence laid the foundation of American industrialization when she endowed the United States with an abundance of natural riches. Her resources of coal, iron, and copper, her oilfields and her forests made her largely self-sufficient for raw materials. Some of the capital she needed came from Europe and so did the bulk of the labor. Responding to the lure of American plenty, immigrants from every part of Europe crossed the Atlantic in unprecedented numbers, thus providing a seemingly inexhaustible reservoir of cheap labor. The federal government's sympathy for business, manifesting itself in its tariff, railroad, and banking legislation, created a climate in which industrial capitalism could flourish. Gifted and ruthless individuals, of whom Rockefeller and Carnegie were the archetypes, created large-scale industrial organizations like Standard Oil and United States Steel, thus removing the uncertainties of unregulated competition and effecting great economies in manufacture and marketing. American science and invention made an equally significant contribution. The inventive genius of men like Thomas A. Edison, Alexander Graham Bell, George Westinghouse, and George Pullman revolutionized transportation, communications, and the processes of manufacture. It also transformed the conditions of life of the American people.

Industrialization was an impressive achievement. But it also had its darker side. Growing too fast to be economically and socially just, it produced great inequalities of wealth, exploitation, class hostility, and a host of complex social problems. The concentration of industry and transportation in the hands of a few led to abuses of power and to a growing demand for the effective regulation of the trusts and other combinations. Labor unrest, the consequence of harsh conditions of work and of the employers' uncompromising hostility to labor unions, erupted periodically in strikes and in terrifying outbreaks of violence. In the cities, meanwhile, the wretched poverty of the new urban slum-dwellers, together with the prevalence of disease, unemployment, and crime, showed that America had not escaped the social ills of industrial Europe.

To critical contemporaries the distinguishing features of the post-Civil War era were materialism, vulgarity, and corruption. Mark Twain called it "the Gilded Age," and the editor, E. L. Godkin, declared that the United States had a "chromo civilization." There was much truth in these criticisms, but the Gilded Age was also an extraordinarily creative period in education, science, thought, letters, and art. Indeed it is hard to think of an age which witnessed so much American accomplishment in the life of the mind. One thinks, for example, of the work of Mark Twain, William Dean Howells, and Henry James in literature; of Charles S. Pierce and William James in philosophy; of Thomas Eakins and Winslow Homer in painting; of Lewis H. Morgan and Willard Gibbs in science.

Political morality stood low in the Gilded Age. Dishonesty and corruption were widespread at all levels of government. Notorious spoilsmen like Boss Tweed and Richard Croker dominated municipal politics, while the Grant administration witnessed a crop of shameful scandals. A succession of second-rate men occupied the presidency and there were few outstanding figures in Congress. But there was more to Gilded Age politics than graft, mediocrity, and drabness. It was an age of intense political excitement, closely fought elections, and impassioned argument over volatile national and local issues. Such critics of the new economic order as Henry George and Edward Bellamy were making their voices heard. More significant still, agrarian discontent was beginning to have political repercussions. The Greenback movement of the late 1870s proved to be the forerunner of the great Populist explosion fifteen years later.

Contents

1 AN INDUSTRIAL NATION   9
The Triumph of Big Business *by B. Supple*   10
A Machine Era *by M. A. Jones*   24

2 THE GILDED AGE   35
Scramble for the Spoils *by J. G. Sproat*   36
Politics of Stalemate *by L. L. Gould*   45

3 THE WORK FORCE   55
The New Americans *by M. A. Jones*   56
Labor on the Move *by R. Jeffreys-Jones*   75

4 A CULTURE IN TRANSITION   86
A Creative Age *by M. Cunliffe*   87

5 THE IMPACT OF CHANGE   105
The Bright Lights of the City *by B. McKelvey*   106
Wealth Against Commonwealth *by M. B. Stokes*   126

BIBLIOGRAPHY   142

Chapter 1

An Industrial Nation

The United States made great economic strides in the years between the Civil War and the end of the nineteenth century. In that period the nation was transformed from a predominantly agricultural society to a manufacturing one, and for thousands of shrewd businessmen there was money to be made—big money. One important factor in this transformation was the readiness of Americans to adapt new inventions—their own and others'—to the needs of industry. The United States by 1900 was the greatest industrial power in the world—a nation more efficient, more affluent, more confident, and more materialistic than ever before.

The Triumph of Big Business

In the last thirty-five years of the nineteenth century—within the lifetime of the survivors of a civil war which had threatened the very existence of the country—the United States became the world's leading economic power. The vast changes which brought this about can only be understood in terms of the transformation of the American business system. For the new society was, more than any other before it, based squarely upon private enterprise. Out of its business system sprang its supreme successes, its gravest defects, its dominant social values, and the major challenges which Americans had to meet.

The United States in the nineteenth century, with an abundance of land and natural resources, depended for her economic growth on an increase in population, which would provide a labor force and a market for her developing production. Between 1865 and 1900, the total population rose from just under 36 million to about 76 million. Most of this represented an increase in native-born Americans, but there was also a large influx of immigrants. By 1900 the foreign-born accounted for more than 13 per cent of the population.

These growing numbers naturally spilled out from the more densely populated East to round out the settlement of the rest of the country. The population of the states in the Midwest, West, and Southwest rose threefold, to about 37 million—almost half the national total in 1900. At the same time the United States began to lose its rural and agricultural character. More and more people moved into the cities to work in industry, commerce, and finance; between 1860 and 1900 the proportion living in towns rose from under 20 per cent to almost 40 per cent. Meanwhile, the number employed in manufacturing, mining, construction, and service occupations increased from just over 4 million in 1860 to over 18 million in 1900. This new America was knit together into a single economy and country with the aid of the telegraph, cheap mail, and, most importantly, the railroad. In the same forty years railroad mileage had multiplied sixfold.

Such changes in the places and ways in which Americans earned a living came with spectacular increases in production. Perhaps the most significant change was the extent of the progress in manufacturing. While agricultural output rose less than three times in the period 1870–1900, that of manufacturing went up sixfold. By the early 1880s the United States had made the crucial transition of modern societies: manufacturing production now exceeded agricultural production. America had also replaced the United Kingdom as the world's leading industrial nation; and by the late 1890s it manufactured about 30 per cent of the world's industrial goods. All this

LITHOGR & PUBL BY KIMMEL & VOIGT 254 & 256 CANAL STR N Y

*Benjamin Franklin, the embodiment of the work ethic,
presides over a representative group of American
craftsmen in this 1873 poster, "By Industry We Thrive."*

stemmed from the high and increasing productivity (output per worker) which characterized American industry. With abundant and varied natural resources, rapid capital accumulation, advanced techniques, and manufacturing organization—in addition to considerable human skills—the output of the average American virtually doubled between 1865 and 1900.

An indication of the efficiency and ingenuity of American industry is the speed with which it accommodated itself to new inventions and discoveries: the typewriter, celluloid, the dynamo, the telephone, electric lighting, the phonograph, the automobile, roll film, and the safety razor, among others. More significant, however, were the new processes and the methods of organization which swept across virtually the whole range of industry. These

provided a mounting flow of coal and iron, steel and textiles, machinery and petroleum products, chemicals and farm equipment, processed food, lumber, and clothing.

At one level these developments encouraged the emergence of new mass-consumption trends in food, drink, and textiles (which together accounted for about 40 per cent of capital in manufacturing industry). These trends resulted from the mechanization and increased scale of plants; the application of assembly-line techniques to meat-packing, canning, and bottling; and the use of new methods, such as refrigeration for food and stitching machinery for boots and shoes. Yet even more important changes took place in the fields which provided goods or services to other industries. The iron and steel and petroleum industries best illustrate these changes.

Modern industrialism was largely built upon iron and steel. They provided its tools and agricultural equipment, its machinery and railroads, its wire and bridges, its pipes and dynamos, its bicycles and automobiles. With spectacular success, American iron production surged towards world supremacy in the postwar years. In the period 1870–1900, for example, the output of pig iron boomed from under 2 million to almost 14 million tons. Much of it was concentrated in Pennsylvania, on the southern shores of Lake Michigan and Lake Erie, and in the Birmingham area of northern Alabama, and in Tennessee. By the mid-1880s the tonnage (principally ore-carrying ships and barges) traveling through the Sault Ste Marie Canal on the way from Lake Superior to Lake Michigan was three times that passing through the Suez Canal.

Big Business in Steel and Petroleum

The United States also registered a resounding success in steel making. (Steel is made from iron by burning out carbon and other impurities to produce a more durable and effective metal.) From a negligible level in 1870 the output of steel rose to more than 10 million tons in 1900 and two years later to 15 million tons. Cheap, multi-purpose, and long-lasting, steel ramified into a host of uses: barbed wire, girders, rods, plates, machinery, tin-plate, pipes, and rails. Steel rails were found by the railroads to be six or seven times more lasting than iron rails.

Under the pressure of an advancing technology, large-scale operation, and a changing market, the steel industry was an excellent example of the general trend to huge plants. The giant Carnegie Homestead plant in Pennsylvania, the largest in the world in 1900, boasted one and a half miles of buildings, used 70 locomotives, and employed 7,000 men. Its various coal mines, coking plants, iron fields, blast furnaces, and steel mills needed complicated transportation and administrative systems. Yet like so much else in the apparently bewildering industrial system of the time, in the last resort all its complexities and perpetual changes led to a simple result. Andrew Carnegie, the self-made millionaire and the greatest steel

In his painting Forging the Shaft *(left), John F. Weir captures the mastery of the machine over the forces of nature. This iron foundry is at Cold Spring, New York. Leaving the "inferno" behind, laborers in Thomas Anshutz's canvas* Steelworkers Noontime *(below) pause for a scrub and bite to eat.*

The industrialist Andrew Carnegie combined the techniques of aggressive selling and large-scale production. As a result of Carnegie's innovations, the United States surged ahead of Britain in the 1890s to become the world's top steel-producing nation. Right: The Homestead plant, near Pittsburgh, was the largest and most advanced of Carnegie's mills.

producer of the age, phrased it as follows:

> Two pounds of ironstone mined upon Lake Superior and transported nine hundred miles to Pittsburgh; one pound and one half of coal, mined and manufactured into coke, and transported to Pittsburgh; one half-pound of lime, mined and transported to Pittsburgh; a small amount of manganese ore mined in Virginia and brought to Pittsburgh—and these four pounds of material manufactured into one pound of steel, *for which the consumer pays one cent.*

If the late nineteenth century confirmed the age of steel, it also anticipated an age of petroleum. The modern petroleum industry dates from the first successful drilling for oil in 1859, which opened up the pioneer Pennsylvania field. In 1870 a mere 5 million barrels were produced, but the figure was 52 million by 1899 when large refineries were operating in Ohio, New York and New Jersey, Pennsylvania, and Indiana. Petroleum products found a ready market in conventional uses: heat, energy, lubrication, medicine, and above all light. As late as 1899 about 60 per cent of the petroleum industry's output went into illuminating oils—primarily the kerosene needed for the lamps of increasingly affluent consumers. But the systems which met these needs—the wells, pipelines, bulk carriers, and refineries—were dramatically new. Nor

was it technological innovation alone which carried the petroleum industry forward.

Extending its activities from refining, Standard Oil (a group of men led by John D. Rockefeller) soon dominated not only the refining, but also the transport and sale of petroleum products. Even in the actual production of crude oil, it controlled a quarter of the national output in 1891. By the 1890s Standard Oil controlled about 80 per cent of the nation's refining capacity. It had reached this position by a combination of matchless organizational and manufacturing efficiency, ruthless competition, and the strategic control of transportation.

The Factors behind Industrial Growth

Much of the thrust of American growth used to be attributed to the Civil War itself. First there was the assumption that war demand and inflation greatly stimulated production, investment, and technological change. Also, growth was believed to have sprung from the success of the North and West which facilitated the freeing of the slaves, high tariff protection to industry, the creation of a national banking system, the passing of the Homestead Act, and land and other grants to transcontinental rail-

Museum of Art, Carnegie Institute, Pittsburgh

Lake Superior region. Between 1860 and 1900 the output of copper rose almost fortyfold.

In line with all this, the westward moving of the frontier of settlement and economic activity continued to be a dynamic element in the process of growth. It provided a flow of food and raw materials to cities and factories; it opened up new outlets for capital investment in farms, mines, housing, schools, railroads, stockyards, processing plants, and roads; it stimulated the expansion of manufacturing and absorbed the resulting products. Yet the role of the frontier should not be exaggerated. The growth of population, the expansion of production, and the rising levels of demand did not exist only at the "official" frontier. Strictly, the frontier comprised a continuous line of territory containing between two and six persons per square mile which in any case disappeared in 1890. The restless ambitions of Americans also created "frontiers" wherever they were.

The most important element in American industrialization was the enormous growth of the market. Its rise could be measured in terms of population, increasing wealth, and the improvement in transportation and communications systems. In contrast to the United Kingdom

Rich in white and Norwegian pine, Minnesota forests churned out 2.5 billion board feet in 1902, the state's peak lumbering year. This photograph shows Minnesota loggers at the turn of the century.

The Bettmann Archive

ways. All of these factors were supposed to have led to rapid economic and industrial growth by providing an encouraging framework for business activity. In fact, however, recent statistics suggest that the growth rate of the economy during the decade 1860–70 was the *lowest* in the nineteenth century; and that there was an actual *decrease* in the productivity of labor in manufacturing in those years. Nor is this really surprising: a prolonged and destructive civil war is hardly apt to prove directly beneficial to the economy.

It was, of course, the South which bore the brunt of the fighting and losses. From 1860 to 1870, output per head fell by about 40 per cent; not until the mid-1880s did southern income per capita regain its 1860 level.

In point of fact, the search for a single cause of the performance of the American economy in this period is fruitless. For one thing, the United States continued to enjoy the supreme advantage of a rich abundance of extremely diversified natural resources, vast amounts of which were now exploited for the first time. Enormous tracts of fertile land were opened to cattle grazing and crop cultivation; farmlands almost tripled between 1850 and 1900. Great timber forests were exploited in the Northwest; giant fields of subterranean oil were discovered in Pennsylvania, Ohio, and Indiana; and seemingly inexhaustible supplies of iron ore were worked in the (which had earlier earned for itself the title "Workshop of the World"), the United States's industrial maturity was largely based on a domestic market.

That the American economy was able to respond so vigorously to the attractions of that market was due to broad social and cultural factors. For market development depended on the mobility of labor and capital, and enterprise—that is, on the ease with which men were able to pursue economic objectives. And this, in turn, grew out of the institutions and attitudes which distinguished the United States. American society placed an extremely high value on material achievement and consequently provided strong incentives to pursue economic success. This was often contrasted with the pursuit of objectives in other societies such as status, leisure, or political achievement. "Business flourishes most," wrote Alfred Marshall, an English economist, "where the aim of the business man is not to shine in elegant society, but to be held in respect by those who are the best judges of his special form of strength. This exclusive devotion to one pursuit involves some loss to the life of the individual, but the constructive economic force which it gives to America at this phase of her development is unique."

There are many other possible reasons for the impressive rate of American industrialization in the late nineteenth century. Progressive change rested not only on technical and tangible elements, but also on nontechnological and nonmaterial factors. These included skills and education, improvements in labor and management, economies of scale, specialization, and the reorganization of commercial and financial as well as manufacturing processes.

Organization and Maturity in Business

In spite of legislation in the field of trade and industry, economic decisions rested primarily in private hands. And economic growth produced a proliferation of business activity: the number of firms grew from 750,000 to more than 1 million between 1880 and 1890 alone. Most of these were fairly small. But the dominant characteristic of business development in the postwar decades was the increased importance of large-scale enterprise.

Railroads were the pioneer example of big business, even in the prewar period. Before the war the New York Central, the Pennsylvania, and the Illinois Central railroads were created. After 1865, expansion and the pressures of competition involved spectacular increases in railroads. New transcontinental systems had been constructed, and by 1903 six "groups" (uniting transportation and financial interests) controlled some 164,600 miles, or over 85 per cent of the national total.

But it was in manufacturing and in coal and oil extraction that the postwar trend to big business had its greatest impact—particularly after the great merger movement at the turn of the century. In 1904 John Moody listed in his book *The Truth About the Trusts* more than 300 industrial combinations, controlling some 5,000 plants; the combined capital was in excess of $7 billion. Of the largest fifty, at least half were reputed to control between 70 and 90 per cent of their respective markets. The top seven consisted of such illustrious business names as US Steel, American Tobacco, General Electric and Westinghouse, American Sugar Refining, Distilling Company of America, International Harvester, and American Can.

What factors had produced this trend to giantism and concentration of capital? Perhaps the principal encouragement to the development of big business was the creation of a mass market on a national scale, although the growth of the market was also stimulated by economic and business changes. The doubling of population in four decades, its growing wealth and increasing concentration in urban areas, the creation of a national railroad and telegraph network—all vastly increased the demand for the products of individual firms and made it worthwhile for them to concentrate their activities. Secondly, the trend towards business growth was based upon the economic advantages of concentrated production: the fall in average costs which accompanied an increase in the scale of manufacturing operations. In some industries technological and organizational changes resulted in production methods capable of manufacturing goods cheaply. This was true when production was geared toward the output of large quantities. The changes included large batch processes, standardized and semiautomatic machinery, assembly lines, application of power, and the minute subdivision and systematization of tasks. These changes added greater efficiency to the manufacturing process. They were inaugurated in such industries as iron and steel, petroleum, chemicals, rubber, electrical equipment, mining and smelting, machinery, and meat-packing.

Yet it was not merely a growth in the size of individual plants that characterized big business. It was also the tendency towards integrated activities embracing many different units of production. Business could achieve considerable savings by integrating the activities of various units—either by combining plants producing the same sort of product or by combining activities at different stages of production. Expenses could be cut in the bulk purchase, handling, or sale of supplies; by coordination and specialization of business activity; and by spreading the administrative and economic costs which came from research, advertising, management, finance, and marketing.

The economic situation of an industry with a number of reasonably large-scale firms often meant that it was

With the rise of the giant corporation, industrial finance came more and more to be concentrated at the Stock Exchange in New York's Wall Street.

profitable simply to organize a merger between corporations. The bankers who were instrumental in channeling capital to corporations also took the lead in forming combinations among them, in order to protect their own investments. By the opening years of the twentieth century the growing influence throughout the business sector of such investment banking firms as J. P. Morgan & Co., Kuhn, Loeb & Co., and Kidder Peabody, and of leading commercial banks, had given rise to the idea of a "money trust." This supposedly characterized a new stage of economic evolution: "financial capitalism." John Pierpont Morgan had already achieved reputation, and great wealth, in this field through his efforts in railroad consolidation during the 1880s. In 1889, on a famous occasion, he lectured various railroad presidents in the library of his home and declared, "We, the railroad

Streamlined efficiency contributed to the growth of American industry. This 1880 diagram shows all stages from slaughter to canning being performed under one roof at a Chicago pork factory.

people, are a set of anarchists, and this is an attempt to substitute law and order for anarchy and might." By the end of the century, and on a rising stock market, the skilled and delicate task of forming mergers and handling the resulting stock-exchange transactions had become a specialized and profitable occupation. Once again, the best, although by no means the only, example in this field was J. P. Morgan. His banking firm was responsible for the formation of Federal Steel (1898), US Steel (1901), International Mercantile Marine (1902), and International Harvester (1902).

Almost immediately after the Civil War there was a movement in some industries towards informal or formal agreements between competitors as to prices and output. But such "pools" suffered because they were not legally binding and because they were vulnerable to outside competition. In contrast to the attempts to share markets, various successful firms were establishing a national reputation on the basis of their growth as single units. In the 1870s and 1880s Gustavus Swift built up a Chicago-based packing and distributing organization of meat

products, making use of refrigeration technology and a national system of branches and agencies. Others were forced to follow, and by the 1890s meat-packing was dominated by the "Big Five": Swift, Armour, Morris, Cudahy, and Schwarzschild & Sulzberger.

Yet in addition to this type of growth, which sometimes involved the acquisition of competitors' firms, the emergence of big business also required new organizational forms and mergers of existing giants. The first real movement towards a full identity of interest among the firms which were already growing rapidly on an individual basis came in the 1880s with the formation of trusts. In these, the stockholders of different corporations deposited their shares with a small group of trustees who thereby could exercise effective control over nominally separate firms and operate them as one huge enterprise. In 1882, Standard Oil, which already dominated the petroleum industry with a loose interlocking federation of firms, formed the first trust to embrace its twenty-six companies and to formalize its legal and administrative position. Others soon followed: in 1884 the American Cottonseed-Oil Trust, in 1885 the National Linseed Oil Trust, and in 1887 the National Lead Trust, the Sugar Refining Company (Trust), and the Distillers' and Cattle Feeders' (or Whiskey) Trust. Each of these controlled over 50 per cent of capacity in its respective industry. So profound was its impact on the public consciousness that the trust, even after it was abandoned as a formal means of organization, gave its name to the language as the term for *all* big business—and another word for monopoly.

Strictly defined, the trust had only a short life in American business history. By the early 1890s individual states (notably New York and Ohio), although powerless to touch interstate combinations directly, had effectively undermined the legal position of the trust device. As a consequence, trusts began rapidly to dissolve themselves. Yet the economic vitality of large-scale enterprise was hardly affected by laws directed against the trusts or monopolies.

Having been denied the loose federation of a legal trust, giant enterprises re-formed as single corporations— usually as holding companies. These were corporations which owned subsidiary corporations and operated under the friendly laws of a particular state; New Jersey, Delaware, and West Virginia were especially hospitable. Among former trusts which became holding companies in the early 1890s were the American Sugar Refining Company, the American Cottonseed-Oil Trust, the National Linseed Oil Company, and the Distilling and Cattle Feeding Company. In addition, entirely new combinations emerged and made use of the device of the holding company. On the other hand, the Standard Oil interests dissolved their trust in 1892 and continued as an informal alliance among a limited number of people. Until 1899

seventeen investors from ten families had a majority of the shares. That year the Standard Oil Company (New Jersey) was formed, holding stock in 41 companies, employing 35,000 people, and controlling almost $300 million of assets.

The formation of the new Standard Oil organization came in the middle of a boom period for such endeavors. Prosperity and rising prices after 1896, the election of McKinley on a probusiness platform in 1896 and 1900, and the accompanying stock market boom—all facilitated a new combination movement. Between 1895 and 1904 there were 313 major industrial mergers involving capitalization of over $6 billion. Over 40 per cent of this was accounted for by the seven largest: Amalgamated Copper, American Smelting & Refining, American Sugar Refining, Consolidated Tobacco, International Mercantile

In his 1889 cartoon "The Rising of the Usurpers and the sinking of the liberties of the people," Thomas Nast strikes at the insidious way in which big business has tarnished high American ideals.

At the banquet held to celebrate the formation of US Steel in 1901, cost was no object. Eighty-nine executives of the eight merging firms (the Carnegie and Federal Steel companies were the major ones) sit in baroque splendor before beginning their feast.

Marine, Standard Oil, and United States Steel.

The United States Steel Corporation—the first billion-dollar company—represented in many ways the changes in American business. The first wave of really huge mergers in iron and steel came in 1898–1900, when there were ten notable combinations. The mergers resulted from a breakup of previous pooling arrangements, the experience of biting competition, the attraction of the industry to financiers, and the forceful activities of the leading businessman, Andrew Carnegie. Even so, the resulting corporate steel giants were not integrated firms; they tended to produce either a single main line of finished output (wire, tubes, tinplate, bridges) or semi-finished steels (crude steel, structural shapes, rails).

But things began to happen in 1900, when Carnegie—a supremely efficient producer of basic steel who was much feared by the rest of the industry—laid plans to construct a giant tube plant on Lake Erie and a railroad from Pittsburgh to the Atlantic. This demoralized the industry and led to a merger which was designed to minimize competition, secure a fully integrated firm, and buy out Carnegie. Significantly, the moving spirit was a financier, J. P. Morgan, who in 1901 organized United States Steel as a merger of mergers, capitalized at $1.4 billion. The new corporation owned 112 lake ore vessels, several railroads, 50,000 acres of coal lands, extensive ore beds, and over 60 per cent of the nation's steel ingot capacity. The underwriting syndicate, managed by Morgan, received a commission of $90.5 million—having expended a mere $28 million in cash. Three Morgan partners moved onto the board of directors. The threat of economic warfare, combined with the profits to be earned from financial management, had created the outstanding industrial giant of the age.

Public Reaction to the Giants

Big business presented two faces to American society. On the one hand, ruthless business techniques and manipulation were combined at times with corruption and even violence to monopolize the market. On the other hand, the use of competitive efficiency and administrative skills had raised productivity and lowered costs for the consumer. Defenders and critics alike tended to see inevitability in the rise of large-scale firms. At the end of the century the corporation lawyer John R. Dos Passos saw big business as "the necessary and natural handmaiden of advancing commerce . . . we should never have reached the colossal developed conditions in which we find ourselves unless the instrumentalities of aggregated wealth had aided it." Taking a more negative view was the novelist Edward Bellamy, whose book *Looking Backward: 2000–1887* (published in 1888) was the most successful fictionalized attack on a system of private trusts. In it he condemned traditional, small-scale capitalists as "totally incompetent to the demands of an age of steam and telegraphs." For him, as for many Socialists, "vast economies" could only be secured "by concentration of management and unity of organization," and in his utopia all industry and trade is concentrated in one gigantic, publicly controlled syndicate: "The epoch of trusts has ended in The Great Trust."

The issue posed by Bellamy—the immense power of large corporations, and the possibility of its misuse in private hands—was one which troubled many contemporaries. Skeptics complained about the unfair use of selective and punitive price cutting, the squeezing out of small competitors by underhand means, stock watering, corporate manipulation and industrial spying, and the bribery of politicians and judges to secure favorable treatment. The object of most criticism in these respects was Standard Oil. As early as 1881 Henry Demarest Lloyd, a crusading journalist and muckraker, attacked the Rockefeller group at Standard for using its power over railroads to secure rebates and thereby undermine competitors. "Their great business capacity would have insured the managers of the Standard success," he wrote, "but the means by which they achieved monopoly was by conspiracy with the railroads."

It is well to emphasize that the balance of opinion favored business enterprise at this time. Expansiveness, practicality, and rapid change were already deeply embedded in the national character and society. The material achievements which were the dominant characteristics of business activity were precisely those which the majority of the nation had come to value. In October 1900, a trade journal, *The Iron Age*, called the period "an age of utility" with new sorts of "genius." The word was used purposefully: among "businessmen and manufacturers to-day are to be found those whose achievements make them worthy to rank with the great men of past generations who wrought only to please the mind or the senses. And among these men of creative and constructive genius the greatest are Americans."

Nevertheless, the economic and technological changes after the Civil War did not have a smooth passage. Apart from the general radical programs of reform movements —the Liberal Republicans of 1872, the Grangers of the 1870s, the Populists of the 1890s—a diffused antitrust movement characterized much of the period. The attack on big business which was the basic theme of this move-

John D. Rockefeller, founder of Standard Oil, was an aggressive monopolist and the nation's first billionaire. Ruthless in his acquisition of small refineries, he was the butt of reformers and cartoonists. Inadequate federal action to curb Rockefeller's monopolistic strength prompted Horace Taylor to create this 1900 cartoon, "What a funny little government." Rockefeller mollycoddles White House staff, while in the background the Capitol maintains Standard output.

Snark

ment was at bottom a reaction to the disruptions of inherited relationships provoked by the rise of large-scale enterprise. Part of the reaction against big business was based on the democratic tradition of American political philosophy—the right of the individual. But the giant, centralized corporation disrupted markets as well as political theories. This fact explains the opposition of many small- or medium-scale entrepreneurs to such businesses as Standard Oil or the American Sugar Refining Company. It explains why the first really virulent opposition to Rockefeller and his associates came from inside rather than outside the petroleum industry. Leading the opposition were rival refiners who wished to reduce the corporation's economic and strategic advantages by legal means, and producers who blamed Standard for the collapse of crude oil prices in the late 1870s. These critics wished to reduce both Standard's control of pipelines and the favorable rates and rebates which it secured from railroads. Their appeal—to the Pennsylvania legislature and to public opinion—was phrased in terms which were to become most familiar. Standard Oil, they said, was a monopolistic concentration of economic power dangerous to the welfare of all Americans, a conspiracy using the power of wealth to beat down competition, ruin other businessmen, and exploit the consumer. Its vaunted economies of operation were based not upon rational organization, but on naked aggression. In the exaggerated words of one trade journal in 1879, "There never has existed in the United States a corporation as soulless, so grasping, so utterly destitute of the sense of commercial responsibility and so damaging to the commercial prosperity of the country as is the Standard Oil Company."

Although the antitrust movement appealed to a wide variety of people including politicians and lawyers, writers and intellectuals, consumers and workers, the mainstream of the antitrust movement derived from interests with more obvious economic grievances. In other industries as well as in petroleum, businessmen felt the economic threat of the trusts. They argued in favor of limiting the effectiveness of combinations in order to expand the opportunities of smaller scale entrepreneurs, appealing to the virtues of competition and to the interests of the consumer. This threat was also felt by farmers—for whom industrialization came as a great material and ideological shock. The agrarian sector—perpetually over-expanding itself into higher debts and lower incomes—grew restive. It pressed for inflationary policies; it felt hostility toward moneyed interests in the East and antipathy toward corporations and monopolies; and it championed local control of economic affairs.

The first business institution to bear the brunt of agrarian discontent was the railroad. Whether they exploited the West through their control of rates and outlets for goods, or facilitated its development—and they undoubtedly did both—railroad companies incurred the wrath of agrarian groups. In one state after another—particularly in Illinois, Wisconsin, Iowa, and Minnesota—a wave of regulatory legislation took place in the 1870s. It was designed to keep down transportation and storage rates and to oversee the railroads by means of permanent commissions. But the principal weakness of such measures lay precisely in their local nature. Like all big business, railroads were interstate organizations; in law or in fact any feasible regulations could only be established on the same basis. In other words, public policy, to be effective, had to be initiated and maintained at the federal level. What transpired in the 1880s was a rising trend to curb private enterprise in railroading on a national basis.

The first major assertion of federal regulating power over private business came in 1887. The Interstate Commerce Act of that year forbade any discrimination in freight rates and prohibited charging higher rates for shorter distances. The act attempted to prevent uncompetitive pooling and ordered that rates be "just and reasonable." Although the Interstate Commerce Commission was set up as a permanent administrative agency for its enforcement, the act was relatively ineffective for many years. Several factors prevented it from being influential, including the continuing opposition of railroad companies and the doubts of the Supreme Court (between 1887 and 1905, of sixteen decisions on cases involving rates, all but one were in favor of the railroads concerned).

By the 1880s, however, the attack on corporations had broadened beyond the railroads. Henry Demarest Lloyd's anti-Standard Oil article "The Story of a Great Monopoly" in the *Atlantic Monthly* of March 1881 precipitated other, more general, attacks on trusts. In 1884 he urged control of combinations on grounds of social morality:

We have given competition its own way, and have found that we are not good enough or wise enough to be trusted with this power of ruining ourselves in the attempt to ruin others . . . we have had an era of national inventions. We now need a renaissance of moral inventions. . . . If our combinations have no morals, they can have no values. If the tendency to combination is irresistible, control of it is imperative. Monopoly and antimonopoly, odious as these words have become to the literary ear, represent the two great tendencies of our time: monopoly, the tendency to combination: antimonopoly, the demand for social control of it. As a man is bent towards business or patriotism, he will negotiate combinations or agitate for laws to regulate them.

As industry after industry experienced increased concentration of economic control, the chorus of criticism in the 1880s—from small businessmen, farmers, labor, and intellectuals—mounted. The fears expressed were as diverse as their origins. Each group had its own perspective. To the farmer, the trusts might represent eastern business dominance and exploitation; to the moralist, abuse of power, political corruption, and the erosion of democratic and egalitarian ideas; to the businessman, unfair and ruthless competition and personal economic loss; to labor, wage restrictions and proletarianization; to the spokesman for the consumer, private control of the means of living. But two themes appear to stand out: anxiety concerning a real or supposed private concentration of power, and reluctance to accept what seemed to be the decreasing opportunities for individuals and small businessmen.

By 1890, twenty-seven states and territories had antitrust laws, and fifteen states had adopted constitutional provisions against monopolies and restraints on competition. Some state action was successful, but this was an exception and in any case merely persuaded combinations to reorganize in different institutional forms. In the last resort there was very little that the states *could* do. As with the railroads, so with industry: big business was an interstate phenomenon; only federal power could reach it.

The desire for national law to check the new national combinations was at last acknowledged in 1890 with the passage of the Sherman Antitrust Act. In brief sentences the Sherman Act declared illegal every monopoly, contract, combination, or conspiracy in restraint of interstate or foreign commerce. It was swept through Congress with the merest token of opposition. Possibly the virtual unanimity reflected as much an absence of real thought on the subject as a recognition that there were serious and complex social problems involved. The act hardly went beyond the common law on monopoly and the restraint of trade judged to be injurious to consumers. In addition, its very simplicity was misleading. Controversy over not only what its framers meant but over what the act itself *should* mean has gone on ceaselessly ever since. In the next decade or so, the Sherman Act turned out to be a very weak device for grappling with new and significant problems. By 1901 only eighteen cases had been taken to court; most of these were trivial and innocuous compared to the more significant instances which the antitrust movement had envisaged in the 1880s and 1890s.

It was not merely judicial interpretations and conservatism which were holding back the course of economic reform. The efficiencies and benefits of big business and large corporations were plain to see by all save a minority of the critics. The difficulty was to identify their evils and propose remedies which would eradicate them without harming the good features of large-scale enterprise. The discussion had not gone far enough to convince a majority of responsible men that they knew precisely what to do in order to eliminate abuses while still allowing the economic good to continue.

Yet as the century drew to a close, the "trust problem" became more acute and discussion of it intensified. After 1896 there was a distinct revival of mergers. As one combination after another was put together, the antitrust movement began for the first time to take a realistic shape and form. It began to affect circles of influence nearer the real seats of power.

This trend was underlined in 1898 when Congress appointed the Industrial Commission to consider the major economic problems of the newly industrialized American economy. Its first report was issued in 1900, and significantly enough it dealt with the subject of industrial combinations. The commission's conclusion was far from novel, yet in the context of the preceding thirty years it represented some official progress: "Experience proves that industrial combinations have become fixtures in our business life. Their power for evil should be destroyed and their means for good preserved." Economic change had proceeded so rapidly—had become so firmly established—that society could not easily return to another business structure. America in 1900 could no longer seriously envisage a drastic reform of its economic system designed to prevent or completely nullify the rise of big business. Quite apart from the risk to the economic benefits which it brought to society, its eradication would have involved a political, social, and economic process too painful to be willingly undertaken. As John R. Dos Passos argued before the commission:

> If corporations were bad, if aggregated capital were pernicious, if it distilled poisons into the veins of the commerce and labor of this country, the time to have acted was to have throttled the corporation in its cradle forty years ago, but now when it is twined around every branch of your commercial development, your industrial prosperity, and your financial body, you are not apt to listen to a demand to destroy it, to cut it down. The destruction of corporation means the end of your present commercial system.

Presented, therefore, with the alternatives of rejecting large-scale private enterprise and inviting upheaval, or accepting a reformed structure and using policy to direct business along beneficial lines, public opinion opted for the latter.

Ushering in the new century, the preliminary report of the Industrial Commission anticipated a period of much more informed criticism and far more concrete public action on the subject of big business. In terms of public policy, the real process of adjustment to big business came only after 1900. Yet the muckrakers, the Progressives, and the policies of presidents Theodore Roosevelt, Taft, and Wilson concerning combinations were merely partial and culminating expressions of the massive social adjustment to industrialization which had begun within a decade of the end of the Civil War.

A Machine Era

One of the features of the economic revolution that followed the Civil War was the flood of inventions and technological innovations that accompanied it. That American industrial technology came in this period to outstrip that of the rest of the world was not because Americans possessed a unique flair for invention. Most of the key scientific discoveries upon which American technology was based had been made by Europeans, sometimes several decades earlier. The principle of the dynamo, for example, had been discovered in 1831 by the British scientist Michael Faraday, half a century before Charles F. Brush of Cleveland, Ohio, began the large-scale manufacture of dynamos in America. The American genius consisted not so much in making new inventions as in applying the discoveries of others to the industrial process.

There were several reasons for American technological leadership. One was the relative scarcity of labor; this encouraged a search for labor-saving devices. Another was the fall in the post-Civil War years in the price of manufactured goods: the consequent narrowing profit margins stimulated the introduction of more efficient techniques. More influential still, perhaps, were the qualities characteristic of Americans. Less tradition-bound than Europeans, more optimistic and adaptable, Americans not only embraced new methods more readily but were impelled by a searching curiosity to seek them out.

The American tradition of technological innovation was not new. It went back to the earliest years of the Republic, if not, indeed, to Benjamin Franklin, who in 1742 invented an improved stove. In 1787, the year the Constitutional Convention met at Philadelphia, a Delaware farmer's son named Oliver Evans built an automatic flour mill. He thus laid the foundation for the system of mass production which, a century later, would make the United States the world's leading industrial power. Evans also improved upon James Watt's steam engine and thus contributed—as did John Fitch, who exhibited his newly invented paddle steamer to the delegates at Philadelphia—to the coming of steam navigation.

The most important American inventor in the years immediately after independence, however, was New England's Eli Whitney. His improved cotton gin made possible large-scale cotton cultivation in the South. But Whitney is even more important for the system he introduced in the manufacture of guns. His method was to make each of the parts to the same precise pattern. This was the origin of the system of interchangeable parts which was crucial to industrial development and mass production. Within a short time the system was being used in clock-making and by the middle of the nineteenth century in the manufacture of sewing machines and other goods.

Indeed, by 1850, the reputation of the United States as the home of invention had already spread abroad. At the Great Exhibition of 1851, held in London to celebrate the superiority of British industry, American inventions like Cyrus Hall McCormick's reaping machine and Samuel Colt's revolver created an immense stir. To perceptive Englishmen such products were a portent of American industrial supremacy. It was already clear that the striking advance of American industry since 1815 owed much to the ingenuity of American inventors and technicians. The decades before the Civil War witnessed a whole series of notable inventions and innovations. In 1839 Charles Goodyear discovered a means of vulcanizing rubber—that is, of eliminating its adhesive properties—and after further experiment developed a uniform product which made possible the growth of the rubber industry. In 1844, Samuel F. B. Morse, hitherto best-known as a portrait painter, revolutionized communications when he transmitted by electric telegraph from Baltimore to Washington the famous greeting "What hath God wrought!" Two years later, Richard M. Hoe invented the first steam cylinder press. By making it possible to print more quickly and more cheaply, he put the newspaper industry on an entirely new basis. In 1846 also, Elias Howe of Massachusetts devised and constructed a successful sewing machine. This was soon afterwards improved by Isaac M. Singer and, when applied to the manufacture of ready-made clothing and shoes, played an important part in equipping the northern armies during the Civil War.

Yet, substantial though they were, these achievements were dwarfed by the extraordinary upsurge of inventiveness that occurred after the Civil War. Some impression of its scale may be gained by noting that the number of patents issued to inventors in the United States jumped from 2,000 a year in the 1850s to more than 13,000 a year in the 1870s and to over 21,000 a year in the 1880s and 1890s. To be sure, many of these patents were for quite trivial improvements; others again were for inventions that proved impracticable; not a few turned out to be hare-brained. But Mark Twain was nevertheless right in regarding the volume of patents as a significant yardstick of national progress. The first official act of his Connecticut Yankee upon assuming the post of Wizard at King Arthur's Court was to establish a patent office. A country without one, he explained, was "just a crab and couldn't travel any way but sideways or backways."

In the last analysis, however, the importance of this rash of postwar discoveries and inventions was not to be measured by their number. Their true significance lay in their impact on everyday life—upon business methods; modes of communication; and travel, dress, entertainment, leisure, and social attitudes. What American inventors did in these years was to create a new civilization, based on the machine. The social and cultural shape of the twentieth century was foreshadowed by what they brought into being.

Of the many mechanical devices which now appeared, none can have done so much to change business life as the typewriter. It was to lead, among other things, to new job opportunities and careers for American women. The inventor of the typewriter was a Milwaukee printer named Christopher Latham Sholes. Having earlier invented a device for printing serially the pages of a book, Sholes came upon an article in the *Scientific American* pointing out how the immense growth of business correspondence had created a need for a quicker, clearer, and more permanent method of keeping business records and writing letters than the use of pen and ink. He then set to work to meet this need and in the autumn of 1867, with the help of some friends, produced a machine from which

A crucial boon to business efficiency was the typewriter. In 1868 Christopher Latham Sholes patented the forerunner (below) of the modern device. It was successful because it typed faster than one could write. The Sholes machine operated on the "understrike" method, whereby depressing the wooden keys (right) caused the slugs inside the wheel to register the character on the paper. E. Remington & Sons (gunmakers) improved, renamed, and marketed the Sholes machine. The Remington "Typewriter No. 10" first appeared on the market in 1908.

the modern typewriter is descended. It had a movable carriage, a lever for moving the paper from line to line, converging typebars, and a keyboard on which the keys were arranged alphabetically. But Sholes's original model was full of defects and it required six more years' work by him and his associates before it was perfected sufficiently to be manufactured.

In 1873 an arrangement was made with the Remington gun company for the manufacture of typewriters on a commercial scale. One of the first purchasers was Mark Twain, who in 1874 gave the new invention the following endorsement, in a letter he typed on his own machine:

> I believe it will print faster than I can write. One may lean back in his chair and work it. It piles an awful stack of words on one page. It doesn't muss things or scatter ink blots around. Of course it saves paper.

The Adventures of Tom Sawyer, which appeared in 1876, is believed to be the first important novel composed on a typewriter. Within a decade there were few American offices without a typewriter. And by then other mechanical devices were appearing to speed the pace of business. The cash register, invented by James S. and John Ritty of Ohio in 1879, and the adding machine, perfected by William S. Burroughs of New York in 1891, became in due course standard office equipment.

An even greater impact on business, and indeed on everyday life, was produced by improvements and inventions in communications. In 1862 the electric telegraph was extended across the continent, and after the Civil War the growth of telegraphy was rapid. By 1878 Western Union, which controlled 80 per cent of the telegraph business, owned 195,000 miles of telegraph routes. A major advance was J. B. Stearns's invention in 1872 of the duplex method whereby two messages could be sent simultaneously in the same direction. Two years later came a further refinement when Thomas Alva Edison invented the quadruplex method. This allowed four messages to be transmitted simultaneously on one wire, that is, two in either direction.

Several attempts to lay a transatlantic cable had been made before the Civil War, but all had ended in failure. Success seemed momentarily to have been achieved in July 1858, when a signal was sent from Ireland to Newfoundland, but after only a few weeks the line went dead. Too high a voltage had been used and the insulation of the cable was ruined. A lack of capital and the outbreak of the Civil War then combined to delay matters for several years. But in 1866 Cyrus W. Field, the retired merchant who had been the moving spirit behind the prewar ventures, at last brought the project to a successful conclusion. The completion of the transatlantic cable to Europe transformed the outlook of Americans. Gone was the former sense of detachment from the Old World. Instead there developed a feeling of intimate contact with Euro-

pean events. News, instead of taking two weeks or more to cross the ocean, was transmitted instantaneously. So too were commodity prices and stock market quotations. American businessmen, arriving for work in the morning, could rely on finding on their desks an up-to-the-minute report on European business conditions.

Within the United States itself nothing did more to expedite communication than the development of the telephone. This epoch-making invention was the work of Alexander Graham Bell, a young Scot who had come to America by way of Canada. The early 1870s found him conducting a school for deaf mutes in Boston, while at the same time toiling away in a basement workshop to "make iron talk," that is, to produce a machine capable of transmitting the human voice electrically. It was not until June 1875, when Bell and his assistant, Thomas A. Watson, heard a faint sound over the wire from the complicated mechanism they had set up, that a practical solution to the problem was found. Thereafter progress was rapid. In March 1876, Bell transmitted the first intelligible complete sentence over a line he had erected between Boston and Cambridgeport, Massachusetts. A year later he was able to converse between Boston and New York, and he and his associates established the Bell Telephone Company for the commercial development of the instrument.

But other claimants contested Bell's rights—a fairly common practice whenever inventions were announced —and it was only in 1879, after protracted litigation, that his claims were upheld. By that time the telephone had already been widely adopted—the Bell Company had installed 56,000 telephones in fifty-five cities, including one in the White House for the use of President Hayes. A long-distance telephone service was begun in 1884; other inventors, among them Edison and Emile Berliner, made improvements to Bell's instrument. By the 1890s, the American Telephone and Telegraph Company, which had been established to run the entire Bell system, had installed nearly half a million instruments in American homes and offices. Service for a time remained expensive: as late as 1900 New Yorkers had to pay $240 a year to rent a private telephone. But the fact remained that, only a quarter of a century after its birth, the telephone was well on the way to becoming an everyday American convenience.

Improvements in transportation were less spectacular than those which brought about the communications revolution. Nevertheless the vast expansion of railroad mileage after 1865 was accompanied by a variety of technological innovations that combined to make travel by rail safer and more comfortable. In the 1840s and 1850s a railway jour-

A combination of scientific curiosity and concern for helping the deaf led in 1875 to Alexander Graham Bell's great invention. Right: Bell places the first phone call between Chicago and New York (1892).

ney was an ordeal. The passengers sat on hard, wooden seats arranged along the sides of closed, box-like cars. They were lucky if they escaped being choked with smoke and showered with sparks from the locomotive, and in winter they risked being frozen as well. Even at the end of the Civil War there had been little improvement. But within a few years, railroad travel had been transformed. The substitution of steel rails for iron and the introduction of wider roadbeds made for a smoother journey. A greater advance still was the appearance of the all-steel car. Wooden cars were a fire hazard and were liable, in the event of an accident, to splinter and cause fearful personal injuries. But the steel car was fireproof and, moreover, infinitely stronger; thus it was not apt to burst apart or telescope in the event of a collision.

Another important contribution to safety was the air brake, invented by the New Yorker George Westinghouse. Until the 1860s train braking was crudely and inexpertly done, often with the result that the passengers would be hurled on to the floor of the carriage. This was because of the absence of a continuous braking mechanism, whereby every wheel could be braked simultaneously. In any case it was extremely difficult to stop a train in motion, and train wrecks were common as a result. It was after examining one such wreck at Schenectady that Westinghouse began working on an air brake. He drew his inspiration from an article on the use of compressed air in the rock drills employed on the Mont Cenis tunnel through the French and Italian Alps.

Westinghouse's invention consisted of a series of reservoirs of compressed air in each car, connected by a continuous pipe running under the entire train to a master reservoir in the locomotive. By means of a device known as the triple valve, the engineer could apply the brakes simultaneously to every wheel and thus bring the train smoothly and speedily to a halt. Tested near Pittsburgh in the fall of 1868, the Westinghouse invention was patented the following year, when the inventor was not yet twenty-three. By 1872 Westinghouse had patented an automatic air brake, so constructed that if a car became detached the brakes set themselves.

Westinghouse's air brake was only one of a number of safety devices adopted by American railroads during this period. The automatic car-coupler, invented by Eli Janney in 1873, obviated the need for a brakeman to go between the cars to link them together. By 1888 Janney's device had become standard equipment on all American railroads. An even greater contribution to safety was the interlocking telegraphic block system, first installed on the Camden and Amboy Railroad by its chief engineer, Ashbel Welch, in 1865. By dividing the track into blocks and allowing only one train in the same block at any given time, the system preserved a safe distance between one train and another.

While the inventions of Westinghouse and others were

Determined to bring an end to the discomfort of train journeys, George M. Pullman patented the sleeper (1863) and later the diner. This 1877 hand-bill beckons prospective customers to travel by Pullman.

making railroad travel safer, an enterprising New Yorker named George M. Pullman sought to make it more comfortable—indeed, to provide it with elements of luxury. That was why, when he incorporated his sleeping car company, he named it the Pullman Palace Car Company. Pullman built his first sleeping cars for the Chicago and Alton Railroad before the Civil War; he simply refitted ordinary railway cars with berths. These proved successful and in 1864 he invested $20,000 in building in Chicago the first real Pullman car. The "Pioneer," as it was known, was an ornately furnished vehicle; it was also a foot wider and two-and-a-half feet higher than regular railroad cars—dimensions that meant it could not travel over an existing railway line.

But Pullman had a great stroke of luck in 1865. After Lincoln's assassination, the United States Government hired the "Pioneer" to carry his body from Chicago to Springfield. This necessitated the modification by one line at least of its protruding station platforms and low bridges, and it brought the Pullman car great publicity. Then General Grant used the "Pioneer" for a trip from Detroit to Galena, Illinois, and a second route had to be adapted to allow it to pass. That began a trend, and when they began to be attached to regular trains in company with old-style sleeping cars, the Pullmans emerged the clear favorites, despite their higher charges. Once the success of his sleeping car was assured, Pullman introduced fresh innovations. In 1867 cooked food became available on trains for the first time, and the following year came the dining car proper—a compartment given over exclusively to providing food. Within a few years, parlor and drawing room cars began to be produced and in 1879 Pullman felt sufficiently established to concentrate car construction at the model town of Pullman, near Chicago.

Closely connected with the growth of railroads was the development of bridge building. Some of the most noteworthy bridges arose in the Middle West, where long bridges were needed to span such mighty rivers as the Ohio, the Mississippi, and the Missouri. The first of the great western structures was the suspension bridge across the Ohio at Cincinnati. Opened in 1867, this was the first American bridge with a span of more than 1,000 feet. Two years later the first bridge over the Missouri was completed at Kansas City, and in 1872 a second was opened linking Omaha and Council Bluffs across the river in Iowa. Even more imposing—and more costly—was James B. Eads's bridge which towered impressively over the Mississippi at St Louis and which was opened to traffic in 1874.

But the most celebrated bridge of all was Brooklyn Bridge—to many Americans the greatest engineering feat of the nineteenth century. The need for a bridge linking Manhattan with Brooklyn had long been evident. Ferryboats had been the only means of crossing the East River, but they were inoperative when the river was frozen. At the close of the Civil War, a wire manufacturer and engi-

The Brooklyn Bridge was the world's longest when it was opened in 1883. The engineer who designed it, John Roebling, had accurately predicted that it would be "a great work of art."

neer from Germany, John A. Roebling, designed a structure to arch the East River. It was a suspension bridge with a main span of 1,595 feet and two side spans, each of 930 feet. This would make it the longest bridge in the world.

Many people doubted whether such a massive bridge could be built. But Roebling, already famous as the architect of the Niagara and Cincinnati bridges, went ahead. In the winter of 1866-67 he sank the first caisson—a watertight chamber used for underwater construction. The work was to take sixteen years and would cost $15 million. Roebling died in 1869 and his son, Washington Roebling, who supervised the construction thereafter, became paralyzed for life as a result of working in the compressed air of the caissons. But he saw the task through and on May 24, 1883, the bridge was opened to traffic by President Arthur in the presence of his cabinet and the justices of the Supreme Court. Brooklyn Bridge was a major milestone in the history of engineering technology, for reasons other than its length. It was the first suspension bridge to use steel-wire cables and one of the first to be built on pneumatic caissons. It was, moreover, as handsome as it was useful. Roebling's design called for the use of 400 wire-rope cables that radiated diagonally from two massive granite towers and from the main suspension cables. This gave the bridge the appearance of a spider's web; it also provided the tension needed to minimize vibration. All the same, Brooklyn Bridge, which was to become one of New York's best-loved landmarks, got off to a tragic start. Six days after it opened, its creaking produced a panic-stricken rush to the shore; twelve people were killed in the pandemonium.

"The Wizard of Menlo Park"

Of all the technological advances of the period, none can have had a wider impact than the use of electricity to provide light and power. That electricity could be a source of light had been proved early in the century: Sir Humphry Davy had demonstrated an arc-lamp powered by batteries to the Royal Society in London as long ago as 1807. But arc-lights were too glaring for general use and too dangerous to be employed indoors. Before electric light could be used for street and home lighting, it needed a vacuum bulb with a durable filament.

This was the problem taken up by Thomas Edison, with whose name the introduction of electricity for light was destined to be indissolubly linked. Born in Ohio in 1847, Edison's rise was not the rags-to-riches story of popular legend: he came from a comfortable background. But he grew up with little formal schooling and became a railway newsboy at the age of twelve and a telegraph operator at sixteen. Even as a youth, Edison was fascinated by the

world of electricity and he devoted all his spare time and cash to technical experiments. In 1869 he patented his first invention, a telegraphic vote-recording machine. He then set up as an inventor and in the course of the next few years devised several improvements in telegraphic apparatus, such as the quadruplex machine, and made other inventions, including a resonator for analyzing sound waves.

By the spring of 1876 he had moved with his laboratory and fifteen of his co-workers to the New Jersey village of Menlo Park. This was an important development in the history of invention. The day of the individualistic inventor was ending. Edison's invention "factory" was based on the concept of team research. He believed that the proper way to approach the problem of invention was not to wait for "discoveries"—flashes of insight which came to scientists exploring problems at random—but to organize them. One should collect a team of highly skilled technicians, provide them with the best possible equipment, and put them to work to supply the market with new products. In short, Edison was driven not by scientific curiosity but by commercial demand. He had no pretensions to being a pure scientist; on the contrary, he generally scoffed at scientific theory—though some knowledge of it would have saved him a lot of time. As it was he preferred to rely on trial-and-error.

In 1877 Edison invented the phonograph, probably his greatest invention. And in later years his laboratories produced scores of new inventions—the storage battery, the fluoroscope, the motion picture projector, and the electric locomotive—and hundreds of improvements. But the achievement which accounted for his immense popular fame was the carbon filament lamp—the first commercially viable product of its kind—which he patented in November, 1879. But Edison did more for electric light than produce a cheap and durable incandescent bulb: he also designed a circuit whose widely distributed outlets were powered from a central station but could be turned on and off independently. The way was now open for the large-scale introduction of electric light. In 1880 Edison installed a complete lighting plant on the newly built steamship Columbia. He then proceeded to build his first American central power station on Manhattan, which went into operation on September 4, 1882. At 3 PM the switch was thrown and the lights went on in eighty-five buildings in the Wall Street financial district. Electric light had arrived, and within six years Americans were using 2 million light bulbs.

There was still much to be done, however, before the electrical revolution was complete. The aim of the Edison Electric Light Company, as its name implied, was simply to provide illumination; it did not attempt to exploit electricity as a source of industrial power. Before that could be done, it would be necessary to find a way of transmitting high voltage electric current over long distances.

Collections of Greenfield Village and the Henry Ford Museum

US Department of the Interior, Edison National Historic Site

Thomas Edison, seen here with an early model of his "talking machine," spent only three months at school. Yet his work resulted in sweeping and permanent changes in American society and made him the nation's best-known inventor. The phonograph later developed the distinctive trumpet-shaped horn of the 1908 model at left; his "Kinetograph" made motion picture shows possible.

That ruled out the Edison Company for it manufactured only direct current, which could not be transmitted for more than about a mile. It was thus left to the inventor of the air brake, George Westinghouse, to demonstrate the superior advantages of alternating current. By using transformers, Westinghouse showed that high voltage alternating current could be transmitted safely over long distances at a comparatively low cost. During the 1880s he and his associates found ways of employing the alternating current system in industry and, thanks also to the development of the dynamo by Charles F. Brush and others, electric motors came rapidly into use in factories.

At about the same time a former assistant of Edison's, electrical engineer Frank J. Sprague, worked out a practical method of using electrical power for urban transportation. The overhead trolley was the invention of a Belgian immigrant in Detroit, Charles J. Van Depoele, but it was Sprague who in 1887 supervised the building of the first electrical streetcar service at Richmond, Virginia. This proved to be so successful that within three years fifty-one cities had adopted this method of transportation, and there were more than 5,000 miles of electric trolley line in operation in the United States.

Gail Borden and George Eastman

At the same time as the birth of the electric age, new technology was changing American food habits. Hitherto diet had been limited by the absence of any effective method of preserving food out of season. That was now to be changed by the development of artificial refrigeration and of canning and concentrating food. Before 1860, fresh meat had been available only at certain seasons; the only way of preserving it had been by salting and smoking. But after the Civil War, meat packers like Gustavus F. Swift and Philip D. Armour developed the railroad refrigerator car as a means of extending the market for fresh meat and of shipping the product the whole year round. The refrigerator car not only made fresh meat continuously available, but in the process reduced its price. It also encouraged new methods in the cultivation of fruit and vegetables, and led to the introduction of new varieties and strains.

The basic principles of canning, that is, of cooking and preserving food in sealed containers, had been discovered by a Frenchman, Nicolas Appert, during the Napoleonic Wars. About the same time, tin cans were patented by an Englishman, Peter Durand. The first American cannery was opened in Boston in 1819. But canning techniques made little progress before the Civil War. Canning remained a slow process, each batch of food requiring to be immersed in water for six hours. But in 1861 the Baltimore canner, Isaac Solomon, discovered a way of speed-

Canning led to more varied and nutritional diets for American consumers. The industry was dominated by Henry John Heinz, who opened his Pittsburgh factory in 1888.

H. J. Heinz Company

ing things up. Using Davy's discovery that the addition of calcium chloride raised the boiling point of water to 240 degrees, he cut the processing time to half an hour. Immediately afterwards, the Civil War created a great demand for canned goods and production rose in a decade from 5 million to some 30 million cans. After the war, mass-production techniques were applied to the manufacture of tin cans; canned fish, meat, tomatoes, corn, and peas were to be seen more and more frequently in American larders.

The inventor of concentrated foods was a retired Texas surveyor named Gail Borden. What led him to take an interest in the problem was the tragedy of the Donner party—the group of California-bound emigrants who were trapped by early winter snows in the Sierra Nevada in 1846 and who had to resort to cannibalism to escape starvation. Borden had personal knowledge of the food problems of pioneers and believed condensation would solve them. He felt that all foodstuffs could be drastically reduced in volume without loss of quality. He declared: "I mean to put a potato in a pillbox, a pumpkin into a tablespoon, the biggest sort of watermelon into a saucer."

Borden's first attempt to put his theories into practice resulted in his manufacturing a "meat biscuit." It was unpalatable and was a commercial failure. He then turned his attention to the product for which his name would become a synonym—condensed milk. The idea of condensing milk came to Borden while he was on his way home from Europe in 1851 after unsuccessfully displaying his meat biscuit at the Great Exhibition in London. He saw how the lack of fresh milk affected the health of immigrant children in the steerage and, on returning to America, moved from Texas to the Shaker community at New Lebanon, New York, there to carry out experimental work on condensing milk. Like other American inventors, Borden was unconcerned with theory; it was Pasteur, and not he, who would later show that it was bacteria (which could be killed by heat) that caused milk to turn sour. Borden relied meanwhile on observation and ingenuity and these proved adequate to his purpose. The key to success proved to be the use of a vacuum pan of the type employed by the Shakers in making sugar. In 1856 Borden patented condensed milk and two years later began manufacturing it. Recent revelations about infected milk in New York and its effect upon infant mortality

An ingenious Shaker technique used to refine sugar inspired Gail Borden's condensed milk process, patented in the 1850s. When this advertisement appeared (1893), Borden's was a household name.

worked to the advantage of the new product, but it was its use by Union soldiers during the Civil War that put Borden's business on a firm basis. Once condensed milk had been successfully launched, its inventor returned to Texas—to the town of Borden—to spend the rest of his life working on processes for concentrating other foods like fruit juices, tea, coffee, and cocoa.

Perhaps the most characteristically American of the many technological innovations of the period was the Kodak camera, invented by George Eastman. This little black box was the means whereby an arcane hobby was so simplified as to become an everyday mass activity. Photography had arrived even before the Civil War. Its impact was enormously increased by the conflict itself, thanks to the work of Mathew Brady and others who took their cameras to the battlefields. But until the 1880s photography was still a complicated and tedious business, daunting to all but the zealots. True, there had been some real improvements since 1865. The introduction of "dry plates" meant that photographs did not, as before, need to be developed as soon as they were taken; hence it was no longer necessary for the photographer to trundle a great mass of bulky equipment around with him in a wheelbarrow. All the same, even dry glass plates were heavy and fragile and were difficult to transport. Because of this, the enthusiast had still to do his own developing, a tricky and time-consuming process.

George Eastman's great contribution was to make skill superfluous. He made it possible for everyone to take snapshots and in addition undertook to develop the exposed film. In 1884 he devised a substitute for glass plates: he hit upon a method of coating paper with gelatin sensitizer and was thus able to produce a roll of "film" that would work inside the camera. Using paper-backed film he marketed his first camera in 1888 under the trademark "Kodak." It was compact, efficient, and absurdly simple to operate. It cost only $25, including the first roll of film and the processing of its one hundred pictures. No longer did the amateur need a dark room and a bath of hyposulfite of soda: he simply sent the exposed film to the Kodak factory to be developed. At first he had to send the camera as well—that is, until 1891, when Eastman introduced a daylight loading film. By such means Eastman brought about a popular revolution in photography, one which was aptly summed up in the words of the famous Kodak advertising slogan: "You press the button—we do the rest."

Thus in the generation after the Civil War a host of techniques, machines, and gadgets transformed the conditions of life in the United States. The leisurely rural Republic of Lincoln's day became the "push-button civilization" of 1900. Understandably enough, Americans were proud of the ingenuity and skill of their inventors and tended to see only the benefits of the new technology. These were numerous and readily apparent: science and technology had simplified and quickened communication, robbed travel of much of its danger, raised living standards, released millions from back-breaking drudgery, extended the horizons and enriched the leisure hours of the common man.

But along with its rewards the new technology brought disadvantages, though these were fully apparent only with the passage of time. The speeding-up of business and of industrial production placed corresponding strains upon the human beings involved: American life became more hectic, the American people more anxiety-prone. Mechanization greatly increased the physical hazards of factory work and produced a sad toll of accidents and injuries. Moreover, by eliminating the need for individual skill, the machine tended to make work monotonously repetitive and to strip it of personal satisfaction and pride of creation. Here, the twentieth century would discover, was drudgery in another form. And as the twentieth century would also learn, technology tended to lessen people's capacity to create their own entertainment. Edison's phonograph not only retired the amateur fiddler and the drawing-room soloist, but brought about the decline of the glee club and the barber-shop quartet.

Kodak Museum

George Eastman House

Inventions and gadgets designed for convenience and pleasure enchanted a growing public. George Eastman created a sensation when in 1888 he produced the "Kodak," so simple that even a child could use it. Left: Eastman in 1890 on board the SS Gallia poses with the Kodak No. 2. Above: The original "Brownie," which appeared in 1900, cost only $1. Its simplicity— and price—made it an instant success.

Chapter 2

THE GILDED AGE

American politics in the late nineteenth century were marked by corruption and stalemate. A grateful nation awarded the presidency to wartime leader Ulysses S. Grant in 1868 and again in 1872, but Grant's political ineptness and ill-judged appointments led to scandals at all levels of government. After 1876, the Democratic and Republican parties were deadlocked. Election battles were closely fought and majorities were small as the politicians argued over tariff and currency reform and how to handle the trusts. The most lasting result of political developments during these years was the firm establishment of the two-party system.

Scramble for the Spoils

At the close of the Civil War, the Republican party appeared to be in a powerful political position. As the party of union and freedom, it took credit for the victory over secession and the abolition of slavery. The economic legislation that a Republican Congress had enacted during the war set the United States on a course it would follow for the remainder of the century. The mood of the American people after the war was one of full-throated nationalism, and the Republicans could claim truthfully to be a party dedicated to economic expansion, free enterprise, and national greatness.

Certain difficulties also beset the party, however, and kept its leaders constantly alert to their vulnerability in national elections. Many Republicans who had come into the party before the war from the ranks of the abolitionists and free-soilers saw their party's mission as completed with the emancipation of the slaves and the restoration of the Union. Although they were not yet ready to abandon their Republicanism with any finality, increasingly during the turmoil of Reconstruction they became restive and began to explore alternative political moorings. As Reconstruction dragged on, moreover, the radicals in Congress lost influence in party affairs. To replace them, a group of tough-minded men emerged in the Senate, whose overriding interest in politics was to further the expansion of the American economy. In close alliance with the nation's business and financial leaders, these politicians scorned the idealism and moral commitment of the radicals, preferring to think of themselves as political "realists." During Grant's presidency, they became known as "stalwart" Republicans for their unswerving commitment to government policies and for their actions on behalf of the business interests. Unabashed spoilsmen, the stalwarts also scorned anything that smacked of political reform. "To the victors belong the spoils," was their battle cry, and they were utterly ruthless in dealing with opponents who sought to stand in their way. Among the more cynical and effective of the stalwarts were Zachariah Chandler, senator from Michigan, and the flamboyant Senator Roscoe Conkling of New York.

As a party, the Republicans continued to draw their major support from industry and labor in the North and from farmers in the Old Northwest. They also benefited immensely until the late 1870s from their appeal to the Negro vote in the reconstructed states of the South. As economic issues arose to replace the issues of the war years, however, the strains on this heterogeneous makeup of the party increased.

As for the Democrats, they seemed particularly vulnerable to defeat in the postwar years. For one thing, they suffered long and grievously from the Republican charge

Speaking of President Ulysses S. Grant, Henry Adams once observed, "A great soldier might be a baby politician." A Civil War hero and the eighteenth president, Grant was criticized for his political favoritism.

Courtesy Chicago Historical Society

that they were the "party of treason and rebellion." For another, they were divided internally and often bitterly over the money question. Some Democrats pressed for a commitment to a "soft money" policy that would keep the economy inflated with wartime paper currency (greenbacks) in the interest of farmers and other debtors. Other Democrats insisted just as firmly that only a "sound money" policy would maintain the fiscal and moral integrity of the nation. These men based their policy upon the assumption that the only real money was money redeemable on demand in gold. Moreover, the Democrats were imbued with a philosophy of states' rights, decentralization, and weak government. They had no program for the nation as a whole to compare with the legislative achievements of the Republicans. Indeed, such programs as they offered had a distinct localist, particularist ring to them. This appeal to localism tapped strong Jacksonian sentiments in millions of voters who were not yet persuaded that strong central government or legislation would necessarily benefit national economic interests. But for all their disabilities, the Democrats remained a strong, if loosely organized, political force.

At their nominating convention in 1868, the Democrats wrote into their platform the inflationary "Ohio idea," calling for payment of the national debt in greenbacks. Then seemingly repudiating their action, they named as their candidate for president the "sound money" governor of New York, Horatio Seymour. Together with his running mate, a states'-rights Missourian, Seymour was thoroughly representative of his party's anti-nationalist orientation and the ticket appealed strongly to the localist sentiments persisting throughout much of the country. Seymour came very near to winning the election, a remarkable feat considering the fact that only three years had elapsed since the end of the bitter Civil War. But in the final count he lost to the man the Republicans had almost automatically nominated at their convention, the great war hero General Ulysses S. Grant.

The Issues Facing Grant

Grant was a political innocent. Only once in his life had he voted for a president, and he knew nothing about national issues beyond a working acquaintance with reconstruction. Nor did he possess the ambition and intellectual vigor to learn about the issues or to master the intricacies of the American political system. For the Republican stalwarts in Congress, however, he was an ideal candidate. They knew that he commanded the respect of the people, who would see him as the right man to lead the nation in a period of change and uncertainty. They knew that he would receive the votes of the Civil War veterans. And they fully expected him, once elected, to become a figurehead president, who would leave the management of the country and the party to them.

The new president's conception of his office was a singular one, owing much to his political naiveté. He regarded the presidency as a reward to him, and to such friends as he chose to designate, for his wartime achievements—a sinecure bestowed by a grateful nation. In such a view, the president functioned chiefly as a ceremonial and symbolic figure, not as a national leader and certainly not as a forceful politician asserting the power of the executive office over the other branches of government. Thus, Grant willingly conceded supremacy to Congress in the formulation of policies and programs, an arrangement that accorded perfectly with the wishes of the stalwarts. Any chief executive at the time, to be sure, would have faced formidable odds in trying to steer an impatient American nation onto a course of responsible economic and social development; but Grant did not make even a feeble attempt to be a responsible national leader.

Only in making appointments did he assert that independence for which he had been noted as a soldier, much to the dismay of the seasoned politicians. In structuring his administration, he behaved as though he were staffing a general headquarters for a military campaign, selecting advisers and cabinet officers more for their personal loyalty and congeniality than for their proven ability. In eight years as president, Grant appointed twenty-five men to the cabinet, and only a bare handful were men of any ability or distinction. To offset his few fortunate choices —Hamilton Fish as secretary of state, Jacob Cox to head the Interior Department, Ebenezer R. Hoar as attorney general—he surrounded himself with mediocre and incompetent men, some of whom ultimately proved to be thoroughly corrupt scoundrels. In an orgy of spoilsmanship, he permitted old wartime comrades, friends and chance acquaintances, and members of his family to swarm into government positions. Increasingly, too, he welcomed the company of unctuous businessmen and smooth-talking politicians, who taxed neither his intelligence nor his judgment. Typical of many Americans at the time, he was inordinately impressed by men of great wealth, and they in turn showered him with gifts and flattery. Although Grant himself was never personally corrupted by the shoddy men he catered to, their influence in his administration made it one of the most corrupt in American history.

The Grant era (1869–77) was a time of great econo-

Both pictures: Library of Congress

Most of Grant's cabinet appointments went to men of no distinction. Two notable exceptions were Secretary of State Hamilton Fish (left) and Attorney General Ebenezer Hoar: both proved to be upright and competent statesmen.

mic significance for the American people. It was the period in which the new middle-class business interests consolidated their wartime gains. It marked the high tide of the age of "free enterprise" and the ascendancy of business interests over agricultural interests. Government policies during these years contributed directly to these developments, especially as they afforded a favorable political climate in which businessmen could operate virtually as they pleased.

A NICE FAMILY PARTY.

*This cartoon refers to Grant's reply on winning
the presidential nomination: "Let us have peace."
After Grant became the new president, political
backers looked to him for government posts.*

Doubtless, the most vexing question to confront Grant was what to do about greenbacks. Should the $430 million in wartime paper currency continue to circulate as legal tender, as inflationists demanded; or should these greenbacks be retired as expeditiously as possible? Debtors wanted to retain, even to increase, the paper money in circulation, while creditors favored a policy of contraction in which the greenbacks, while being slowly retired, would be redeemable in gold. Grant supported the "sound money" position, although both he and Republican leaders in Congress were disposed to move slowly in dealing with the problem so as not to upset the economy with any drastic action. In 1869 Congress repudiated the "Ohio idea" and committed the government to the payment of its own obligations in gold. Shortly thereafter, the Supreme Court in a split decision provoked controversy and confusion by ruling that greenbacks could not

be considered legal tender for most debts. The decision satisfied no one, least of all Grant. Fortunately, he was soon able to make two new appointments to the high tribunal. When the Court reversed itself on the question in 1871, the switch could not have come as a surprise to him.

Still, the problem rankled; indeed, the money question persisted as a volatile political issue until the end of the century. During the Panic of 1873 the government reluctantly raised the amount of greenbacks in circulation as a means of dealing with widespread unemployment and unrest. Two years later, the Resumption Act provided for the exchange of gold dollars for greenbacks and created a gold reserve, in effect making the paper money equal in value to gold. It solved the immediate problem, but it came as a shock to currency reformers who detested the paper money and faulted Grant for equivocating on the issue.

Almost as troublesome as the currency question was the problem of taxes. In reaction to the high levies enacted during the war, Congress by 1870 abolished all wartime excises except those on tobacco and liquor. Two years later, it quietly buried the income tax. But nothing was done to bring down the high tariffs on imports. The wartime legislation establishing the high rates had described them as "temporary duties" only. By the 1870s, however, a powerful constituency in support of permanent high tariffs had developed among entrepreneurs who benefited from the protected market. Indeed, for some manufacturers and their political spokesmen, the principle of protection became almost a religion. Organized lobbies in Washington maintained a watchdog interest in tax legislation and kept Congress under heavy pressure to maintain high duties. Gradually, the effect of the high tariff was to push up the prices of the goods farmers and small businessmen had to pay abroad and lower their market prices at home. This growing imbalance in the economy worked directly to the advantage of the manufacturing interests, but it contributed to rising unrest especially among westerners. Spokesmen for protection insisted that high tariffs benefited the American worker by shielding him from foreign competition. Grant's essential sympathy with the protectionists and with big business in general contributed to a steady rise in tariff rates during his early years in office.

A Clear Need for Reform

Civil service reform was an issue Grant could not entirely avoid confronting. The cause of political reform had been gathering momentum since the war, particularly among a group of educated, well-bred politicians, journalists, scholars, and businessmen—the "best men," as they often called themselves. Their goal was nothing less than the destruction of the spoils system through the substitution of a merit system for the ancient and, as they saw it, dishonorable practice of political patronage. Appointments to government positions, they argued, should be made on the basis of fitness, as determined by competitive examinations.

In 1871 Grant took a significant step in favor of reform when he appointed a Civil Service Commission and instructed it to establish a merit system. Even more encouraging, he named the reformer George William Curtis to head the body. For a brief moment, Curtis and the reformers appeared to have the president's support as they worked against heavy odds to achieve their goal. But pressure from the spoilsmen in the Senate soon pushed Grant back from his bold step forward, and before the end of his first term the Civil Service Commission had perished from neglect and lack of funding. Reformers never forgave him for his retreat on an issue they considered vital to the health of the political system. Moreover, they were totally repelled by the manner in which he treated the friends of reform within his official family.

In 1870 Grant squeezed Attorney General Hoar out of his cabinet to appease the stalwarts, then invited his reform-minded commissioner of internal revenue, David A. Wells, to leave also.

Although little evidence of outright corruption in government surfaced during Grant's first term, the gold scandal of 1869 indicated how easily unscrupulous men could exploit the president's naiveté for their own fraudulent purposes. The incident raised serious doubts in the minds of reformers, especially, about the integrity of the administration. In a bold scheme to corner gold, two notorious speculators, Jay Gould and "Jubilee Jim" Fisk, set out to buy up all the gold for sale in the money market, drive up its price, then sell out at a huge profit to themselves. To succeed, they had somehow to prevent the Treasury from selling government gold in the market during their manipulations. Working through Grant's brother-in-law, they persuaded the president to withhold gold sales temporarily on the grounds that he was helping western farmers maintain high prices for their produce. On September 24, or "Black Friday" as it was called, their manipulations drove up the price of gold to a ridiculously high level and sent the stock exchange into a panic. At last realizing that he had been duped, Grant quickly released enough gold to break the price and foil the conspiracy. But the crisis left many businessmen and investors ruined and the stock market badly shaken.

By 1872, a growing dissatisfaction with Grant in many quarters emboldened some Republicans to challenge his bid for a second term in office. Within the party itself, deep fissures had opened between the president's men— the stalwarts—and other Republicans who resented their dominance. The continued rankling of the southern problem alarmed many people, especially reformers, who wanted to put a swift end to reconstruction and thus remove an impediment to other reforms. Grant's unwillingness to lead and his bungling of civil service reform convinced many prominent citizens that nothing could be done with him in office, either to purify the political system or to deal responsibly with such problems as taxes and currency. Among reformers in general, the suspicion grew that corrosive influences were at work within the administration, corrupting the political process and endangering the nation's honor and integrity. Throughout the spring, the dissidents tried to head off Grant's renomination, but the stalwarts easily thwarted them and made clear their intention to keep the president in office for another four years. Unwilling to go over to the still suspect and discredited Democrats, the frustrated dissidents directly challenged Grant's men by forming a new party, the Liberal Republicans.

Liberal Republicanism, thus, was a movement to rid the Republican party of Grantism, not to alter permanently the two-party system in America. It was also far from a pure reform movement, for many Liberals were interested chiefly in promoting their own political fortunes at the expense of the stalwarts. The party appealed to a wondrous array of dissatisfied voters: reformers and spoilsmen, protectionists and free traders, conservative patricians from New England and agrarian radicals from the West, champions of Negro rights and southern white supremacists. All that united the delegates to its convention in May was a dislike of Grant and a determination to deny him a second term. As one Liberal Republican observed, Grant's failure as president was "a pitiful story, one of the most pitiful in political history." But there was little agreement among the delegates as to the precise nature of his failure.

Given its diverse composition, the party was bound to write an equivocal platform that straddled the issues and contained something to displease everyone. Moreover, in choosing a presidential candidate, the Liberals passed over their strongest reform leaders in favor of the eccentric and controversial New York editor Horace Greeley. That decision alone was enough to send many disgusted

dissidents hurrying back to the regular party. Hoping to take advantage of the dissension among the Republicans, the Democrats at their convention entered into an uneasy alliance with the Liberals and endorsed Greeley, despite his reputation as a harsh critic of everything the Democratic party stood for.

Greeley campaigned vigorously but hopelessly. If the election of 1872 demonstrated nothing else, it proved convincingly that the Republican alliance of politicians and big businessmen had become a powerful political force. With a well-disciplined machine and a huge campaign fund, the regular Republicans had no trouble dominating the campaign, even with the loss of the dissenters. Liberals cried that the nation was in grave danger, but Republican orators made them sound foolish by reminding voters that peace and prosperity prevailed throughout the land. For all his faults, Grant was still the national hero, while Greeley was an easy target for ridicule and satire. "I was assailed so bitterly," Greeley lamented at the campaign's end, "that I hardly knew whether I was running for the Presidency or the penitentiary." Grant rolled up a landslide victory, and within weeks of the election Greeley died, broken in spirit and health. The decision, seemingly, was a resounding mandate for more Grantism, whether or not the voters understood its implications.

Scandals Rock the Administration

Even before the voters went to the polls in 1872, however, the Crédit Mobilier scandal afforded an insight to those who wished to look into the prevailing state of public morality. In September, a New York newspaper revealed the existence of widespread corruption in the building of the transcontinental railroad. The corruption was directly attributable to the laxity of the government in controlling the public funds it had provided for the great project. To build the eastern half of the road, the Union Pacific Railroad had created a dummy construction company, the Crédit Mobilier, through which the directors then siphoned off huge profits, including much of the government grants. To protect their scheme from legislative snooping, moreover, the directors had judiciously distributed blocks of stock among key members of Congress.

Founder and outspoken editor of the New York Tribune, *Horace Greeley (left) was one of Grant's harshest critics. Greeley was the presidential candidate of both the Democrats and the Liberal Republicans in 1872, but owing to his impulsive and eccentric personality he lost the race to Grant. Right: With Grant as their "ringleader," acrobats in the circus of political corruption perform their act.*

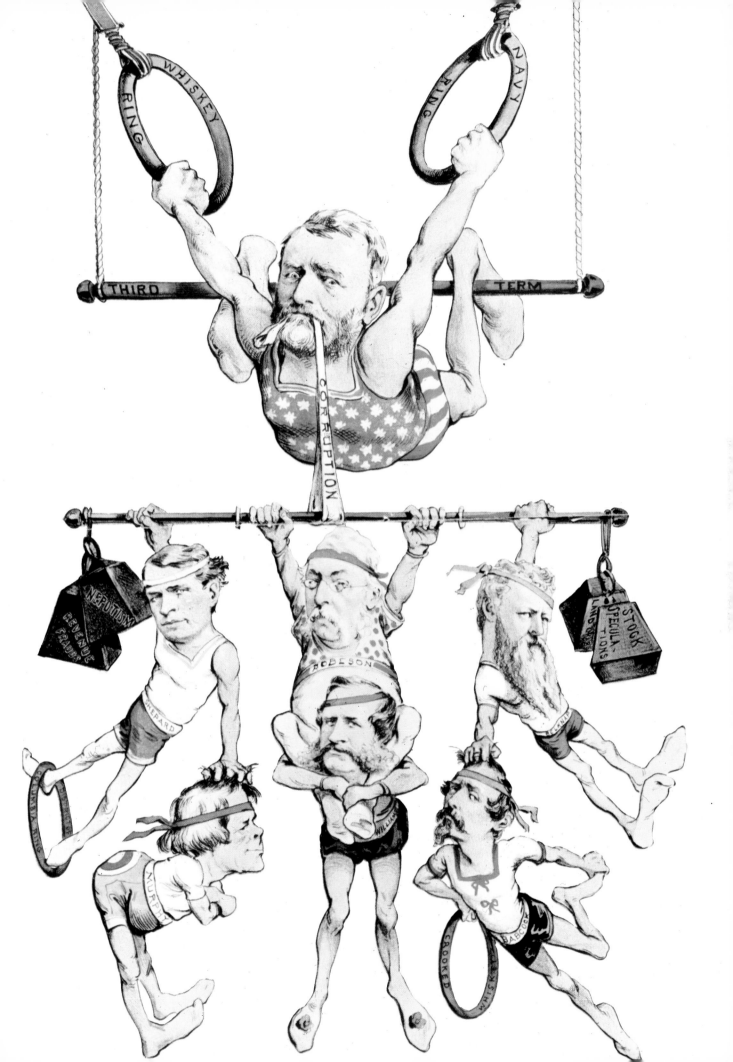

Never was bribery of the federal government carried on so blatantly or on such a lavish scale, as the Crédit Mobilier annually spent some half a million dollars for "public relations" in Washington. Pressure from the newspapers forced Congress to investigate the scandal, and the inquiry ultimately implicated such leading Republicans as Vice President Schuyler Colfax and Congressman James A. Garfield. But while the revelations momentarily shocked the nation, the financial intricacies of the scheme probably only confused the average American citizen. In any event, the matter was never fully and honestly resolved.

Congress provided the people with an issue they could more readily comprehend when, early in 1873, it passed an act which came to be known as the "Salary Grab." This legislation authorized a doubling of the president's salary and awarded the senators and representatives a handsome 50 per cent pay raise as well. The measure was legitimate enough, but an unfriendly press labeled it a raid on the Treasury and public outrage forced repeal of the raise for Congress within a year. In the congressional elections of 1874, the Democrats won control of the House of Representatives. Doubtless, they benefited from voter reaction to the Panic of 1873, a serious economic crisis marked by widespread unemployment; but the victory was also an indication that many voters were unhappy with the recent behavior of Congress.

Within the Grant administration itself, a series of scandals unfolded with devastating impact during the second term. In 1875, Treasury investigators uncovered the "Whiskey Ring," a conspiracy to defraud the government of revenues from the tax on liquor sales. Directed by Benjamin H. Bristow, Grant's third secretary of the treasury and one of his better appointees, the inquiry revealed that distillers and federal agents in St Louis had made off with millions of dollars. "Let no guilty man escape," Grant told Bristow, as evidence of fraud poured into Washington. But Bristow soon discovered that a key operative in the ring was none other than the president's private secretary and old friend General Orville Babcock. As in the gold corner fiasco, Grant once again had allowed himself to be put in a compromising and highly embarrassing position. But this time, rather than move to correct the wrong, he came to the defense of the culprit. When Babcock and 238 other alleged conspirators were indicted by a grand jury, the president intervened directly on behalf of his friend and managed to keep him out of prison. He also undercut Bristow's position and forced that able official to resign from the cabinet.

Next came a major scandal in the War Department. Secretary of War William W. Belknap was discovered to have taken bribes over a period of five years from a corrupt trader in Indian territory. The House of Representatives voted to impeach Belknap; but before the Senate could bring him to trial he resigned, with Grant's blessing, and Congress backed away from further action against him.

The historian and social critic Henry Adams once observed that national politics in the postwar years produced nothing but damaged reputations. His indictment was overdrawn, of course; but the political record of the Grant administration was indeed a dismal one. Grant did not cause the corruption within the national government, nor did he profit personally from the wrongdoings. To be sure, he came perilously close to compromising his honor by permitting his friends and associates to use him in their shady schemes. But any occupant of the White House at the time would have found it difficult, if not impossible, to immunize his administration against the epidemic corruption in American society at large. Americans had become infatuated with a great game of accumulating money, land, material possessions of any sort—and the game had no rules. One historian described the postwar scene as a "great barbecue," at which the greedy guests gorged themselves on the profits of unrestrained economic expansion. Not all Americans crowded to the table, of course, and many tried desperately to maintain traditional values and established rules of conduct. But the pursuit of wealth for its own sake and by any means became an accepted part of the American creed. No one understood what had happened better than Mark Twain, who in his sardonic fashion caught perfectly the spirit of the age: "Get money. Get it quickly. Get it in abundance. Get it in prodigious abundance. Get it dishonestly if you can, honestly if you must."

In such an atmosphere, dishonesty and corruption flourished in both public affairs and private enterprise. Indeed, a close and often unholy alliance between big business and politics was chiefly responsible for the general debasement of morality in the period. Many businessmen regarded politicians, especially city officials and state legislators, as their paid representatives. In return for favorable legislation and administration, business leaders provided the "oil" (that is, money) to keep the political machines running. Simply by contributing large amounts of money to the parties or to individual politicians, the business interests established claims on the political system that they did not hesitate to exploit when the need arose. In state after state, the legislators bowed to the demands of businessmen, sometimes in a sincere belief that they were contributing to economic progress, but all too often in supine response to corrupt pressures. A motion reportedly was once introduced in the Pennsylvania legislature calling for adjournment, "unless the Pennsylvania Railroad has some more business for us to transact."

The most notorious of the corrupt political machines in America's cities was New York City's Tweed Ring. Starting as a volunteer fireman, William M. Tweed worked his way up in politics to become, by 1868, the "boss" of the

"Boss" Tweed and his Ring

In the late 1860s, New York City was being systematically robbed of millions of dollars by William Marcy Tweed and his notorious Ring. "Boss" Tweed and his henchmen, including City Chamberlain Peter Barr Sweeny (or "$weeny") and City Comptroller "Slippery Dick" Connolly, elevated graft to the status of an art through their control of the New York City Democratic political machine—Tammany Hall. Their masterpiece—and downfall—was the county courthouse.

The original appropriation for the building of the courthouse was $250,000 including all the furnishings. Tweed insisted that such a sum would not allow for a building which could suitably reflect the city's pride and the law's majesty. He persuaded the Board of Supervisors to add $1 million more, then another $800,000, then $300,000 more, and another $300,000, and later another $500,000. By 1871, with the building still not finished, more than $13 million had been spent.

By now many people had begun to ask questions, including the *New York Times*. Their investigations revealed that the money was all accounted for—in warrants drawn by Comptroller Connolly and signed by Mayor A. Oakley Hall, another Tweed crony.

These warrants made fascinating reading. Carpets, they revealed, had cost the taxpayer $350,000. Questioned about this sum, the supplier said: "There is one thing you people down in the *Times* don't seem to take into account; the carpets in these public buildings need to be changed a great deal oftener than in private houses." Plumbing and gas light fixtures cost $1.5 million. Lumber and carpentry came to $800,000—mostly for doors and window frames in the marble building. And later the carpenter received another $800,000 for repairing and altering the same woodwork! Similarly, $500,000 was spent on plastering, and $1 million on repairing the same plastering a year later while the building was still incomplete. Door locks consumed $2,700; safes $400,000; awnings $24,000; three tables and forty chairs $180,000. "Brooms, etc." cost exactly $41,190.95 and stationery $186,000. One check for several thousand dollars, made payable to Fillippo Donaruma, was endorsed "Philip F. Dummey"; in several cases the dates on which payments were recorded turned out to have been Sundays.

The procedure for making these payments was simple. Each contractor submitted a grossly inflated bill for his work, knowing that he would receive 35 per cent of the total. The other 65 per cent

Cartoonist Thomas Nast lambasted Tweed and his henchmen. Below: The Tweed Ring. Below right: Vulture Tweed intones "Let us prey."

was delivered by "Slippery Dick" to the Tweed Ring. When rumors of this procedure leaked out, the Board of Supervisors quickly established an investigating committee to examine its own dealings. Later an independent Special Committee to Investigate the Courthouse was set up by the city fathers to investigate *this* committee. The special committee's report revealed no wrongdoing, but the members had obviously learned a great deal: they promptly submitted their own bill for $18,470.35—for twelve days' work.

Investigating committees may not have worried Tweed, but he never managed to control the *New York Times*. The newspaper ran a series of articles in 1871 detailing the most infamous wrongdoings of Tammany Hall. And if Tweed was annoyed with the *Times*, he was furious with Thomas Nast's crusading cartoons which appeared regularly in *Harper's Weekly*. Nast refused an offer of $500,000 to study art abroad rather than corruption at home. "I don't care a straw for newspaper articles," lamented Tweed, "my constituents can't read, but they can't help seeing them damn pictures." The Boss was right. The pictures were seen and Tweed died in jail in 1878.

The courthouse was the most notorious of the Tweed Ring's many shady deals and it made Tweed and Tammany Hall synonymous with the most blatant and pervasive political corruption. But the Boss never repented. When he entered prison, the warden asked him his profession and Tweed promptly replied, "Statesman!"

city. Tweed accumulated power by systematizing the corruption in the larger economic system, through an elaborate system of payoffs and kickbacks on contracts, franchises, and services. Everything done in New York City involved a kickback to Tweed and his associates. Public buildings were constructed at fabulously padded prices, often in collusion with supposedly honest contractors. On one incredible occasion, New York's city hall was actually sold to a private bidder to satisfy a claim against the city; then it was bought back for more than the amount of the first sale. With his colorful crew of henchmen, "Boss" Tweed over the years plundered the city of an estimated $100 million, a staggering figure. His downfall resulted only because his corrupt practices became too flagrant for the city's "respectable" citizens. Alarmed by the city's precarious credit rating in the international money markets, local business leaders decided that Tweed's "bossism" had become too costly. Thus, he was driven out by a reform coalition led by the prominent lawyer Samuel J. Tilden. But his political machine only faltered momentarily before recovering its power. Corruption became less obvious in the city's government without Tweed, but it continued unabated.

Even in its foreign affairs, the United States could not escape a taint of corruption in the postwar era. Succumbing again to the bad advice of scheming friends, including his secretary Babcock, Grant gave his approval to a dubious plan to annex the island of Santo Domingo. Economic interests on the island were eager for annexation, hoping that the move would bolster their positions, and they were encouraged in their plans by a group of disreputable American speculators. Although he knew nothing of the scheming, Grant was fascinated by the notion of expansion and tried to force a treaty of annexation through the Senate. But the chairman of the Foreign Relations Committee, Senator Charles Sumner, denounced the treaty and blocked its passage. Infuriated, Grant pressured his stalwart supporters into removing Sumner from his chairmanship, but he was unable to revive the plan.

In other respects, the Grant administration performed well in its conduct of foreign relations. Secretary of State Fish was an able, if conventional and colorless, diplomat whose most constructive achievement was the easing of strained relations between the United States and Great Britain. Friction had developed during the war, when, according to the Americans, the British government had violated international law by allowing Confederate raiders to be built and armed in England. Subsequent American demands that the British pay for damages to Union shipping caused by these raiders had long been resisted in London. In 1871 Fish negotiated the Treaty of Washington, which provided that all outstanding differences between the two countries be submitted to an international tribunal for arbitration. When the tribunal decided in favor of the United States, the British accepted the decision and a

Even Grant's war record could not salvage his prospects of nomination for a third term. This 1880 cartoon, "Grant As His Own Iconoclast," shows how the president had lost the nation's respect.

delicate situation was peaceably resolved. Other differences between the two nations were also satisfactorily compromised through international arbitration. Indeed, the Treaty of Washington was a landmark in the history of international cooperation for the settlement of disputes among nations.

Ironically, Grant anticipated the judgment of history on his presidency. In an extraordinary last annual message to Congress, he reviewed his administration and confessed its failings in domestic politics. "It was my fortune, or misfortune," he acknowledged, somewhat pathetically, "to be called to the office of Chief Executive without any previous training." Mistakes had been made, he noted, but they resulted from errors of judgment, not of intent. He also spoke with pride of his record in foreign affairs, noting that "the United States has been happily free during the past year from the complications and embarrassments which have surrounded some of the foreign powers."

It was a fair assessment. Grant contributed to the difficulties of his presidency through the flaws in his character and temperament, to be sure. But he was more a victim of time and circumstances than a willful instrument of misgovernment. He was also, in his way, a representative president, who reflected the good intentions and flawed performance of American society in general. Certainly he never lost his popularity; and with all the graft and scandal that surrounded him, there were strong third-term movements for him in 1876 and 1880.

Politics of Stalemate

For fifteen years after the election of 1876 the American political system experienced intense partisan competition and vigorous electoral combat as the evenly matched Republicans and Democrats struggled for supremacy. In an era that followed party politics closely, responsible leaders dealt with serious issues and proposed solutions to the problems of an industrializing and urbanizing nation. The Gilded Age was, in its public life, far more than a drab, sordid display of corruption and mediocrity. It was a robust and creative period from which emerged political alignments and issues that would extend into the early twentieth century.

The overriding condition that confronted national party leaders from the mid-1870s onward was the existence of a stalemate. After Grant's decisive victory in 1872, the Republican party did not secure a popular majority in a presidential election until William McKinley's success in 1896. Of the GOP's three victories between 1876 and 1892, only James A. Garfield in 1880 won even a narrow plurality of the ballots. The Democrats controlled both houses of Congress for two years between 1872 and 1895; the Republicans managed the feat for only four years in the same period. In hotly contested states like Ohio, Indiana, or Illinois, small percentage shifts in the number voting or in the size of a party's vote could swing an election.

Deadlock was not uniform across the country. The South was throwing off the last vestiges of Reconstruction and Republicanism and settling down to nine decades of emotional devotion to the Democrats. The 135 electoral votes from below the Mason-Dixon line gave Democratic candidates a predictable running start in presidential battles. Republicans were not quite as entrenched in New England, but the area usually went for the GOP. From New York, across the Midwest, to the states of the Great Plains, however, the political struggle was usually heated and close—with victory rarely certain for either side.

The politics of even balance were carried on in a social environment that differed significantly in custom and practice from the setting of public life a century later.

The close elections of the 1870s and 1880s reflected the electorate's intense preoccupation with politics. Eastman Johnson's 1887 canvas shows a good-natured debate in Nantucket, Massachusetts.

Americans devoted immense amounts of energy to political warfare in the Gilded Age. They listened avidly to long, detailed speeches on the tariff or the civil service, standing in the hot sun or sweltering in canvas tents. They read extensive newspaper reports of congressional debates or party conventions and expected a coverage of factional maneuvering that no modern journalist would tolerate. Some of this popular interest reflected the national passion for games and spectacles. But on a more basic level it demonstrated the nineteenth-century citizen's faith in his society and his desire to affect its future.

Most of all, Americans expressed their fascination with politics at the ballot box. Many in society, especially blacks and women, could not vote, but white males with the franchise exercised it at a far higher rate than modern elections ever achieve. Turnout in the North in the 1880s ran over 80 per cent, and 95 per cent of the eligible voters in five midwestern states came out in 1896. Local elections regularly reached 60 per cent, and sometimes even higher. Voting did not exhaust citizen participation in the process of governing. A marked proportion of the electorate took part in party affairs. "We love our parties as we love our churches and our families," observed a New England senator in 1885. "We are a part of them."

The presidency was the capstone of the electoral process, but the chief executive had far less power than his successors in the twentieth century. Custom restrained his functions. It was undignified for him to campaign for reelection and unfitting for him to be excessively absent from Washington. As only the first citizen and not a monarch, the president should not be surrounded with protectors or so aloof that ordinary Americans could not see him in his office or at regular public receptions. He might suggest but could not command, might persuade but must not dictate. "The executive department of a republic like ours," wrote a senator, "should be subordinate to the legislative department." This distrust of executive authority reached back to the revolutionary past, and had only gradually diminished in the first three-quarters of the nineteenth century. Abraham Lincoln had lifted the office out of disrepute, only to have Andrew Johnson and Grant discredit it again. A national position in an age of localism, the presidency would slowly gain in stature as the century drew to an end.

The Gilded Age of Politics

It was to Congress that most Americans looked for leadership on policy questions in this period. The branch of government closest to the people, Congress accepted the doctrine of legislative supremacy as no more than its due. If representatives or senators went to see the president, recalled Senator George Frisbie Hoar of Massachusetts, "it was to give, not to receive advice." But the legislative branch had institutional and political handicaps that restricted its effectiveness. Neither party was able to control the two houses for an extended period; consequently, sustained programs never appeared. Outdated and clumsy rules hamstrung the House. Inflated egos and posturing rhetoric slowed the Senate. It was a struggle to pass the appropriation bills each year, and a debate on tariff or currency legislation could tie down the Congress for an entire session. "Congressional Government," as Woodrow Wilson described it in his 1885 book of that title, was adequate enough as long as society judged government on what it prevented rather than on what it achieved. When it became a question of shaping programs to meet social ills, power would begin to flow from Congress and toward the White House.

Politics had such a central place in American society in the late nineteenth century that its professional practitioners had to expend large amounts of effort on both the management of the party structure and the waging of election campaigns. These twin demands entailed the raising of money and the allocation of patronage, activities that have often been labeled "corruption." Some of the illegal activities involved were simply the informal ways that Americans have always financed politics or influenced the legislative process. Other examples of corruption grew out of the fresh opportunities of an expanding economy, where the lines between the private and the public interest were not clearly defined. By the end of the century reforms like the secret ballot and a more austere popular mood would eliminate many of the vote-counting indignities. The nation would have less success in limiting corporate influence or making campaigns themselves more pure, and these problems would persist for almost a century.

The distribution of patronage, or the "spoils system," had ramifications that transcended the crass aspects of bestowing government jobs on party workers for loyalty to the organization. In a period of intense partisanship, appointment as postmaster of a community, selection as federal district attorney, or nomination to the diplomatic service was tangible evidence of an individual's place in the party hierarchy. A carefully balanced and graded process of reward and encouragement, patronage could in skillful hands knit a party together. Politicians knew that successful management of the spoils was a time-consuming business, and they often wearied of the endless round of place hunters, or what Grover Cleveland called "this dreadful, frightful, damnable office-seeking." But it could not be ignored or mishandled without weakening the party, as maladroit presidents like Cleveland and Benjamin Harrison discovered to their cost.

A British critic of American politics in the Gilded Age, Lord Bryce, wrote that the two national parties "were like two bottles. Each bore a label denoting the kind of liquor it contained, but each was empty." Bryce was wrong. Important issues and ideas separated the Republican and Democratic parties. They appealed to different kinds of voters and presented divergent programs to the nation.

The Political Balance Sheet

The Democrats in the era of Grover Cleveland were the champions of weak government, limited power, and localism. As one leader noted: "It is better for some things to be done imperfectly and clumsily than to set up a paternalistic and bureaucratic government to do them." From this guiding assumption flowed an antipathy to the use of governmental power to promote economic growth through protective tariffs or federal subsidies. For Democrats, said the governor of Massachusetts, "government is a power to protect and encourage men to make the most of themselves, and not something for men to make the most out of." The Democrats were faithful to their dogmatic adherence to states' rights and negativism. They as yet saw no need to alter their principles to adjust to an industrializing nation.

Their electoral strengths reinforced the philosophical commitments of the Democrats. They controlled the House of Representatives for sixteen of the twenty years after 1874, and gained a plurality in four out of five presidential elections after 1872. Democratic dominance in the states of the South and the sectional border, where the race issue made the party ascendant, gave it a secure base from which to assault GOP strongholds. Throughout the nation the Democratic hospitality to racism attracted those who saw the Republican party as too sympathetic to the black cause. Democratic emphasis on economic government wooed men to whom GOP policies seemed extravagant and costly. The religious moralism of many northern Republicans, expressed in prohibition and Sabbatarian campaigns, drove Catholic, German Lutheran, and other ethnic voters of a nonpietistic persuasion into the arms of the Democrats. Tolerance on such explosive questions was a distinct asset at a time when ethnic and cultural issues divided local communities and determined voting as sharply as economic or class considerations. As a political entity the Democratic coalition was diffuse, contradictory, and essentially negative, "little more than a collective grievance."

The Democrats were unable, however, to transform their principles and their electoral popularity into national political supremacy. Chronic internal bickering held them back. The Democratic party, concluded one Republican, was "a hopeless assortment of discordant differences, as incapable of positive action as it is capable of infinite clamor." Party doctrine stressed individualism; individual

Democrats therefore resisted discipline and unity. Focused on the community and on the state, Democratic organizations shrank from coherent party action and produced few national leaders. On the tariff, the most persistent economic issue of the period, the party was divided and confused. Doctrinaires wanted "reform" that would lower customs rates and appeal to consumers with lower prices; professionals knew that reductions on foreign goods that competed with domestic products could be politically disastrous. The resulting tariff straddle symbolized the perennial disarray of the Democrats.

Despite its record of success up to 1876, and its hold on the presidency for all but eight years between 1861 and 1913, the Republican party remained in a far more vulnerable position than its rival during the Gilded Age. Continuing efforts to challenge the Democratic mastery of the South proved unavailing, and left the GOP very much a sectional organization. In the Middle West, where the party's hold was rarely secure, controversies over religious issues, sparked by the moralism of local Republicans, caused a marked slippage in electoral support in the late 1870s. By the end of the decade the issues of the Civil War and Reconstruction were losing their impact as the North abandoned the Negro. Grant's scandals had stained the Republican reputation for morality, and the party had serious internal stresses. A former Republican wrote in 1878 that the GOP "lies wallowing in the mire of its apostasy, the helpless victim of its leaders and the spectacle of the nation."

Party assets offset many of these weaknesses. From its successful prosecution of the Civil War the GOP had gained an identification with the nation that campaign orators used for four decades following it. "The Republican party had saved the Union," wrote one senator's wife. "It was the Union." Democrats called this "waving the bloody shirt," after one Republican speaker literally did so by displaying a bullet-torn Union tunic on the stump. This charge overlooked how long and how blatantly southern Democrats did the same thing with Rebel memories, and how much the recollections of the war represented a genuine reservoir of Republican support. The end of the war, Republicans contended, had not meant an end to their party's record of achievement. Unlike the Democrats, they argued, it was "the party that does things, instead of one that opposes them." Years of power also fostered the development of national spokesmen like James G. Blaine, Benjamin Harrison, and William McKinley, and gave the GOP a generous quota of internal cohesion. The Democrats, recalled a Washington correspondent, were a "headless, undisciplined force," the Republicans, "an organized, well-disciplined army."

What set the Republicans apart from the Democrats was their willingness to employ governmental power and authority to shape the future of society. The protective tariff, "the sacred temple" of the party, best represented the GOP commitment to an active government. High customs duties to protect native industry and agriculture from foreign competition, Republicans argued, would foster business enterprise, safeguard the jobs of American workers, and advance the national interest against other countries. Supporters of the tariff, most notably James G. Blaine, believed that a basic harmony of interest existed among all classes and that protection would benefit all levels of society. Fidelity to protection did not mean that the GOP was simply the party of "Big Business." On the tariff question, it spoke for many in the business community, but not all. More important, the tariff had nationalistic and patriotic overtones that transcended its economic appeal. So too Republican doctrine advocated the use of governmental machinery to create a better and more prosperous society, one which would embrace religious, social, and economic goals.

The Hayes Years

From 1877 to 1892 the dominant theme of party history was the Republican effort to build a national political majority. This campaign began with some success during the presidency of Rutherford B. Hayes. A party moderate from Ohio, Hayes displayed qualities of integrity and discretion which offset the tawdry memories of the Grant years. He reasserted the authority of his office in several well-publicized tests with Congress and restored some of his party's morale. As Hayes confronted the problems of public policy in the Gilded Age, he gained a measure of respect that contrasted strikingly with the controversy that clouded his inauguration in 1877. Observers brushed aside taunts about "His Fraudulency" and concluded that "Mr. Hayes is a remarkably cool hand."

To strengthen GOP claims as a national organization, Hayes pursued a conciliatory approach toward the South designed to foster well-based Republican parties there. In view of growing northern boredom with the reconstruction issues, this policy had compelling partisan appeal, but it did mean the virtual abandonment of blacks to the uncertain mercies of southern whites. The choice of a southern Democrat for a cabinet appointment (ex-Confederate David Key as postmaster general) and the selection of sympathetic regional figures for patronage posts did not soften Democratic resistance to Republican inroads on the South. By the time Hayes left office the goal of encouraging a viable southern Republican party was dead, even though successive GOP presidents toyed with this problem into the next century.

Unhappiness with the conduct of party politics, especially among genteel intellectuals or "Mugwumps" of the Northeast, made civil service reform a vexing problem for the Hayes administration. The president did not share the Mugwumps' elitism, contempt for politicians, or distrust of democracy. But he did see that restriction of congressional prerogatives on the spoils would strengthen his own office and enhance the tone of public life. "We must be relieved," he said, "of congressional dictation as to appointments." In celebrated confrontations over civil service reform with New York's florid Republican senator, Roscoe Conkling, Hayes eventually won most of what he sought. He kept in motion the forces that would lead to reform legislation under his successors.

As the nation emerged from the hard times of the 1870s, the future of the currency system presented perplexing questions for Hayes and his party. Proponents of gold saw attempts to depart from a single standard of value as a threat to financial stability and a menace to the country's monetary relations with the world. Gold seemed to these men the money of respectability, morality, and order.

In opposition to the advocates of gold were the laborers, tradesmen, and farmers, mostly from the Midwest, who supported other forms of currency: greenbacks and silver. Chief among the advocates of silver was the inflationist (and one-time greenback supporter) Congressman Richard Parks Bland. Inflationist efforts led to the enactment, over a veto from Hayes, of the Bland-Allison Act in 1878. This act provided that the Treasury should purchase $2 million to $4 million of silver every month to be minted into silver dollars—equal in value to gold-based currency. Although it placated the inflationists of the Midwest, the act was not very effective. For more than a decade a succession of secretaries of the Treasury insisted on purchasing the minimum amount of silver, thus decreasing its value against the gold-based dollar. Nevertheless it served as a quietening measure until the 1890s when the depression in the South and the West brought the white metal again to the center of American politics.

A Decade of Turmoil

Hayes had committed himself to only one term in office, but his creditable record combined with the shortcomings of the Democrats gave the Republicans a fighting chance in the election of 1880. Despite victories in the congressional elections of 1878 that led to control of both houses of Congress, the Democrats still lacked an attractive national candidate. After booms for Samuel J. Tilden and Horatio Seymour faltered because of the ill health of both hopefuls, the party chose a former general and political novice, Winfield Scott Hancock. He was, observed the New York *Sun*, "a good man weighing 250 pounds." When Hancock told an interviewer that he regarded the tariff as a "local question," he revealed his naiveté as a candidate, allowed the GOP to exploit protection as an issue, and led a cartoonist to portray him asking a political

associate: "Who is Tariff, and why is he for revenue only?"

Republicans had to sort out the conflicting claims of Blaine, Grant, and other presidential aspirants, but finally settled on Congressman James A. Garfield of Ohio. It was a shrewd choice. A persuasive orator and an effective legislator, Garfield had the potential to build on the legacy of Hayes. In the campaign both he and James G. Blaine emphasized the tariff issue after GOP losses in the Maine senatorial election. This decision anticipated the way the tariff would become the centerpiece of the Republican creed in the 1880s. Garfield having won the nomination, the election resulted in a narrow Republican plurality of 10,000 popular votes, reflecting the persisting partisan deadlock, but a more decisive margin in the electoral college.

In its brief months of existence the Garfield administration gave some promise of future achievement. The president defeated Senator Conkling and the localism he represented in a patronage quarrel in the spring and summer of 1881. At the same time, Blaine as secretary of state sketched a "grand design to develop a stable Latin America oriented toward the United States." An imbroglio in Chile clouded Blaine's effort, and the attempt on Garfield's life in July clearly retarded the momentum that the GOP had acquired since 1877. When Garfield died in September, his vice president, Chester Alan Arthur, became president. For the next decade the Republicans struggled to regain a sense of purpose and direction.

Unlike many Republicans of his vintage, President James A. Garfield (above left) did not confer favors willy-nilly. On July 2, 1881, a disappointed office seeker, Charles J. Guiteau, shot the president. Garfield was confined to bed while doctors tried unsuccessfully to locate and remove the bullet. Sapped of his strength, the president died on September 19, 1881. Left: The shots were fired in the waiting room of a Washington train station.

the nation's economic expansion. It was a combination that captivated the party's rank and file.

Blaine's nomination enabled the GOP to wage a vigorous campaign for the presidency in 1884. Yet the Democrats focused their campaign on Blaine's personal character, thereby preventing the Republican hopeful from concentrating fully on the tariff. Nonetheless Blaine's personal canvass of the Midwest, a relative novelty in presidential races, his advocacy of protection, and his popularity were more significant than bolting Mugwumps or a clergyman's indiscreet comment that the Democrats were the party of "Rum, Romanism and Rebellion." Blaine lost narrowly to Democrat Grover Cleveland, but he slowed the party's electoral slide and created an opportunity for the Republicans to rebound in 1888.

Grover Cleveland led the Democrats to victory in 1884 and shaped the party's destiny for the next dozen years. Cleveland had risen rapidly from the obscurity of a Buffalo, New York, law practice to become mayor of that

The day Garfield died, Chester A. Arthur (left) was sworn in as president. He lacked congressional support and failed to get the nomination in 1884. His Democratic successor, Grover Cleveland (below), was dubbed "His Obstinacy" for refusing to confer political favors.

Chester Alan Arthur was a competent executive. In his single term Congress passed the Pendleton Act (1883) that created a civil service system, thereby ending the practice of assessing campaign contributions from federal employees. Yet the disputes of the Arthur years over scandals in the Post Office and a presidential veto of pork-barrel legislation (designed to favor political patronage) dissipated the cohesion that the 1880 election had brought to the GOP. The congressional elections of 1882 produced sizable Democratic gains in the Midwest and Northeast, and portended Republican defeat in the next presidential contest.

As their standard-bearer in 1884 the Republicans selected the most popular party leader of his time, James G. Blaine. Sometimes indiscreet in management of his personal finances, "the man from Maine" was a complex, magnetic politician whose devoted friends called themselves "Blainiacs" and whose bitter enemies accused him of corruption or worse. Contrary to the legends that have made him a vaguely disreputable and obscure figure, Blaine was a constructive nationalist who used the tariff issue to pull his party back together in the 1880s. In speeches and in public letters he sounded the merits of protection as a policy both to win votes and to encourage

The lyrics accompanying this cartoon are: "Ma! Ma! Where's my pa?/ Gone to the White House/ Ha! Ha! Ha!" When rumors during the 1884 campaign suggested that nominee Grover Cleveland had fathered an illegitimate child, he amazed his public by owning up to the fact. The smear campaign backfired and the hero of honesty became the twenty-second president.

city and then governor of New York in 1882. To a party lusting for a fresh face, the stocky Cleveland, whom relatives called "Uncle Jumbo," presented a palatable blend of rugged honesty, conservative views, and a reputation for independence. Despite the Republican revelation during the 1884 campaign that he was the father of an illegitimate child, for which he accepted responsibility, Cleveland still managed to enter the White House in March 1885. On the day Cleveland took the oath of office Democrats celebrated their return to power in the inaugural parade. Cleveland was less exultant than his partisan supporters. "I look upon the four years next to come," he confided to a friend, "as a dreadful self-inflicted penance for the good of my country." In its tone of self-righteousness and implicit self-advertisement, Cleveland's remark forecast the troubles that the new president would face as a political leader.

Successful as a national candidate, Cleveland revealed severe drawbacks as a party manager that troubled his first term moderately and made his second presidency a disaster for his party. Between 1885 and 1889—his first term—he established that his party could govern effectively and gained grudging respect from his opponents. In his relations with fellow Democrats, however, Cleveland was insensitive to the nuances of patronage. At first he was loath to grant positions to loyal party members, and by the time he finally relented and replaced existing Republican officeholders with Democrats, he had systematically alienated the men—of both parties—through whom a president had to work. By the end of his first term Cleveland was the object of acerbic criticism within his party. "Faithlessness is a passport to recognition by this mass of presidential fat," concluded a California Democrat. In a larger sense he failed to revitalize the Democrats. At the same time the GOP was reasserting itself under Blaine and Benjamin Harrison.

There were definite indications during Cleveland's tenure in office that the social quiet that had marked the early 1880s was breaking down. Railroad strikes in the Southwest, early signs of agrarian unrest, and the Haymarket Riot in Chicago in 1886 revealed the stresses and tensions of an industrializing economy. By the middle of the decade the railroad question was a pressure point for many dissatisfied groups. Farmers criticized high freight rates and sectional discriminations. Shippers chafed at the uncertainty which an unstable rate-structure caused. Some railroad men preferred general legislation from Congress to regulation by the individual states, but wanted

*Benjamin Harrison (above) had a presidential record
of diligence. "I am sure we have never had a man
in the White House," his solicitor general once said,
"who was more conscientiously seeking to do his duty."*

at all events to conclude the rate wars and stock fights that characterized the rail business.

The outcome of these diverse forces was the bipartisan Interstate Commerce Act of 1887. The act was designed to regulate rates so that they were "reasonable and just" and prevent local discrimination. It also gave birth to the Interstate Commerce Commission, which had the authority to oversee interstate railroads and to cause any violators of the act to "cease and desist" from unlawful procedure. However, the decisions of the ICC could not be enforced until the issue at hand reached the federal court. The ICC would not assert significant power until after 1900, but the device of the national regulatory agency became significant as the characteristic American response to managing the economy.

Republican gains in the congressional election of 1886 were modest and the prospects looked good for Cleveland's

reelection in 1888. The president attempted to set a ringing theme for the campaign in late 1887 when he directed the entirety of his annual message to Congress to the subject of tariff reform. Because of the surplus in the Treasury, and because lower tariffs would reduce consumer prices, Cleveland advocated a decreased tariff. Protectionist Republicans welcomed debate on the issue but the Democrats were divided. Cleveland and his party retreated from the debate after the Mills bill of July 1888, allowing for minimal tariff reductions, was passed by the House. Had they been more adamant in their stance they could have made persuasive appeals to consumers, importers, and farmers. With customary ineptness, however, the Democrats backed and filled, and whatever unity the tariff message had evoked was gone when the campaign began. The party's performance in the contest itself was equally lamentable. Cleveland took little part even in a supervisory way, and the Democratic managers were proponents of a higher tariff: Democratic policy became anybody's guess. Compared to the energy of their opponents, the Democrats were sluggish and leaderless. A visitor to party headquarters in October reported: "They have washed fully as much as they will hang out."

Republicans Sweep Back with a Vengeance

For their part the Republicans took up the challenge of Cleveland's tariff attack and made it the cornerstone of their effort. They chose as their candidate Benjamin Harrison from Indiana, a spokesman for protection. They put together a well-organized appeal that combined the fervor of the traditional military form of campaigning with the extensive publicity of the emerging new style of elections. Harrison spoke to crowds from his front porch, but this was not done from laziness or indifference. There the candidate could "reach voters in a controlled situation that retained the trappings of spontaneity." Harrison's speeches, and the pamphlets they became, were so effective that a GOP manager wired him: "Keep at it, you're making votes." Republican unity and cohesion, the tariff issue, and Harrison himself gave the party victory in November 1888. Cleveland gained a lead in the popular vote, based on the one-party South, but Harrison won 233 electoral votes as compared to 168 for the Democrat.

The most influential law in the long term of the Fifty-first Congress was the Sherman Antitrust Act. By the end of the 1880s Americans watched in "a state of apprehension, almost amounting to alarm" the spread of large corporations. Congress responded to the complaints of small entrepreneurs, agrarians, and the victims of specific trusts with a bill that prohibited contracts, combinations, or conspiracies "in restraint of trade or commerce." Not rigorously enforced until the twentieth century, the

Sherman Act went as far as the majority wished and farther than any other industrial nation had gone to check big business.

During the congressional session of 1889–90, Harrison and Blaine made some tentative gestures toward a larger world role for the nation. The first Pan American conference (1889) and the reciprocity clauses of the McKinley Tariff both pointed to American interest in expanded trade and improved hemispheric relations. Despite a record of achievement in Congress and the administration's foreign policy overtures, the Republicans were in trouble as the election of 1890 approached. President Harrison was a cold, aloof leader whose frigid manner and inept appointments ate away at party unity. As Speaker Reed wryly noted: "I had but two enemies in Maine. One of them Harrison pardoned out of the penitentiary, and the other he appointed collector of Portland." Democrats exploited deftly racist appeals against the Federal Elections Bill, or the "Force Bill" as they inaccu-

rately called it; they associated the McKinley Tariff Act with higher consumer prices and labeled the legislative body the "Billion Dollar Congress," as it was extravagant and profligate.

Local problems in the Midwest compounded the GOP's national troubles. Republican proponents of programs like prohibition and regulation of religious education moved against their social adversaries in Iowa, Wisconsin, Illinois, and elsewhere. Wisconsin's Bennett Law, calling for compulsory education in schools that used English, aroused the ire of German Lutherans and Catholics. The law symbolized the cultural conflict such measures evoked. Democrats told the voters "the Bennett law is a local manifestation of settled Republican policy of paternalism." Caught between national and local discontent, menaced with rising farm unrest, the Republicans suffered badly in 1890. The number of GOP congressmen fell from 166 to 88; the resurgent Democrats held 235 seats. Republican hopes for a national majority had received a severe jolt.

This toy scale appeared during the 1888 election campaign. The majority of the voters chose Cleveland (right), but Harrison (left) won the electoral college vote and became the next president.

The presidential election of 1892 confirmed the Democrats' revival. Despite a last, half-hearted challenge from Blaine, President Harrison won the Republican nomination. The party loyally supported the incumbent, but the enthusiasm of 1888 had disappeared. "Well," said Reed, "perhaps he is as good a man to get licked with as anybody." Hoping to inhabit the White House a second time, Grover Cleveland remained his party's only national figure and secured a third nomination with relative ease. In a lackluster campaign Cleveland won a 400,000-vote majority, carrying previously staunch Republican states like Wisconsin and Illinois, and leading his party to control of both houses of Congress. As the Democrats sang, it was "Grover, Grover, Four more years of Grover," and the *New York Times* predicted: "No Republican can even hope to see his party again in power for a long term of years."

Dispirited Republicans found the result in 1892 hard to bear. The nation had apparently rejected the GOP's economic nationalism and governmental activism. The Republican attempt "to mold America in their own vision of the good society" had been rebuffed. Democratic caution seemed to the voters more safe and prudent than Republican innovation.

The politics of stalemate were about to end, but the Democrats would not be the ultimate victors. A few months after the second inauguration of Cleveland in March 1893 the nation plunged into one of the worst depressions in its history. Over the next two years Cleveland mishandled the currency and tariff questions. At the same time Democratic cohesion eroded with squabbles over patronage and policy, while in the southern and western Democratic strongholds the Populist party was making damaging inroads. The impact of hard times overshadowed ethnic and cultural allegiances to the Democrats, and the voters directed their grievances once more to the GOP. In the congressional elections of 1894 the Republicans scored sweeping gains and laid the basis for an electoral dominance which would endure until 1929. The bitter battles of the 1890s would change the shape and direction of national politics, and they would make party warfare in the age of stalemate seem quaint and old-fashioned by comparison. This historical judgment, however understandable, was unfair to a period when politics and politicians engaged the energies of much of the populace, confronted real social problems, and saw the emergence, for good or ill, of the two-party system which has dominated the public life of the nation ever since.

From a painting by Joseph Klir (1892), this print of The Lost Bet *refers to Cleveland's second presidential victory. The winner of the bet rides triumphant, drawn by a sheepish Harrison supporter.*

Chapter 3

THE WORK FORCE

A tidal wave of immigrants flooded American shores in the last two decades of the nineteenth century. These newcomers were mostly southern and eastern Europeans who had been forced by a severe depression to leave their homelands and seek new jobs in the expanding United States economy. But frequently the new workers were forced to accept the dismal, low-paid factory jobs of a newly industrial nation. The working conditions in those factories, together with demands for a fairer share of America's industrial wealth for laborers, contributed to the rise of trade unionism. And the new American Federation of Labor, by rejecting political action, ultimately made the trade union movement respectable.

The New Americans

Between the Civil War and the First World War the United States became a mecca for half the world. Week in, week out, during this peaceful half-century the high-funnelled immigrant steamers from Liverpool, Hamburg, and Naples disgorged their human cargoes upon the American shore. In a seemingly endless stream a sizable segment of the Old World's poor marched hopefully down the gangplank at New York's Castle Garden or Ellis Island to begin a new life.

Americans had already experienced the impact of mass immigration; the midcentury influx of Irishmen and Germans had dwarfed anything that had gone before. But now, in the post-Civil War years, with the expansion of the American economy and the improvement of transportation facilities, immigration rose to undreamt-of levels. The total number of new arrivals in the half-century after 1865 was more than 26 million—five times as many as in the preceding fifty years and three times as many as in the previous two-and-a-half centuries. To put the matter another way, this huge migration meant that every week for fifty years the United States opened its doors to 10,000 newcomers. Not that the flow was uniform. Increasing steadily during the 1870s, immigration reached new levels in the following decade, fell off during the depression of the 1890s, and then soared to a peak in the early years of the twentieth century before being halted by the outbreak of the First World War. The all-time record was set in 1907, when there were 1,285,349 arrivals. The immigration statistics were, however, somewhat misleading, for an appreciable number of those counted as immigrants were "repeaters"—international commuters who shuttled back and forth across the Atlantic. Some of them eventually went back to their homelands to live. Nevertheless it seems likely that well over 20 million stayed permanently in the United States.

Until almost the end of the century the great majority of immigrants came from those parts of northern and western Europe which ever since colonial days had

In his lantern slide the artist has carefully included the hallmarks of immigrant arrival: Ellis Island, the footlockers, the American flag, and, of course, the Statue of Liberty.

supplied America with the bulk of her population—Great Britain, Ireland, Germany, and Scandinavia. But in the 1890s there was a significant shift. The number of immigrants from northern and western Europe began to decline, while there was a dramatic increase in arrivals from southern and eastern Europe, particularly from Italy, Austria-Hungary, and Russia. By 1914 more than four-fifths of those who crossed the Atlantic to America were coming from southern and eastern Europe and from Asia Minor. This "new" immigration brought to the United States a great variety of unfamiliar types: Poles, Ukrainians, Lithuanians, Croats, Slovaks, and other Slavic groups; Russian, Polish, and Rumanian Jews; Italians, Greeks, Turks, and Syrians; Hungarians, Armenians, and Finns. And while this motley throng was making its way across the Atlantic, a smaller but still significant movement was in progress from across the Pacific, first of Chinese, then of Japanese and Filipinos. Simultaneously there was a sizable overland influx from the Western Hemisphere, consisting mainly of Mexicans and Canadians.

Contemporary observers tended to draw sharp distinctions between "new" immigrants and "old." They assumed that the shift in the geographical origins of immigration after 1890 had brought about a fundamental change in its character. It was believed that there was something novel, even unnatural, about the new immigration. Not only, it was argued, were there greater dissimilarities in culture and outlook between the newcomers and those among whom they settled, but the new immigration was inspired by more materialistic motives than had animated earlier comers. Indeed, it had been artificially induced by self-seeking business interests. The immigration of northern and western Europeans was said to have been voluntary, spontaneous, and self-directed, and to have been undertaken, at least in part, in a spirit of idealism. On the other hand, that of southern and eastern Europeans was alleged to have been the result mainly of the recruitment efforts of steamship companies, railroads, and manufacturers. As for the immigrants themselves, they had been motivated simply by the desire to make money.

This line of argument was widely accepted. It contributed at the time to the growth of restrictionist sentiment and, later, it influenced the historical treatment of immigration. Yet it was either wrong or misleading. It would be idle to deny that the new immigration, considered as a whole, differed in many respects from the old. The new immigrants came from the most backward parts of Europe. They were generally poorer, less literate, less skilled than their predecessors. There was a higher proportion of single men among them and they were more likely to be "birds of passage." There were religious differences too. Whereas the old immigration had been divided fairly equally between Protestant and

Catholic, later comers were overwhelmingly Catholic, Jewish, or Greek Orthodox. Then again, the political experience of the new immigrants was not as extensive as that of the old. Many of them had been the subjects of despotic monarchs and knew nothing of representative government.

But what was true in general could be false in particular. Thus while the Irish were acknowledged to have been part of the old immigration, they possessed very few of its essential attributes. Conversely, though east European Jews were nominally new immigrants, they had little in common with most groups to whom that designation commonly applied. It was misleading, therefore, to lump together in two arbitrarily chosen categories, diverse ethnic groups who happened to have arrived in the United States at the same time.

The Forces Promoting Immigration

Nor was there any truth in the view that the new immigration was the product of artificial stimulation by business interests. Thus railroads which wanted to dispose of their landholdings played no part in generating the new immigration. They concentrated their promotional activities almost exclusively on the more affluent parts of Europe—Great Britain, Germany, Sweden—and here they achieved significant results. But the only sizable group of purchasers they found in southern and eastern Europe were the Russo-German Mennonites who settled on Santa Fe lands in Kansas in the 1870s. It was a myth also that American industrialists imported vast numbers of unskilled laborers on contract from southern and eastern Europe. They had no need to: the new immigrants came in sufficient numbers without enticement or the promise of a job. Steamship companies, on the other hand, did make great efforts to drum up custom. Each of the great transatlantic lines—Cunard, White Star, North German Lloyd, Hamburg-Amerika—employed an army of agents in Italy, Austria-Hungary, and the Balkans. But like their counterparts in those countries from which the old immigration had come, these agents were employed not to persuade Europeans to leave, but simply to sell tickets to those who had already decided to do so. The encouragement of emigration was strictly forbidden by European governments, and little evidence has been found to substantiate the allegation that steamship agents made systematic attempts to impress the peasants with the belief that employment at high wages was readily obtainable in the United States.

All the same the new immigration was greatly facilitated by the expansion of transatlantic services. Hitherto the way to America from southern and eastern Europe had been long and difficult. But competition between the steamship companies for the lucrative immigrant traffic brought new opportunities for crossing the Atlantic. Companies vied with each other in offering cheap fares, in arranging special trains to ports of embarkation, and in establishing direct services to the United States from Mediterranean ports. Steamship rivalry also contributed to the expansion of the prepaid passage system. By 1890 each line had an elaborate network of American agencies offering passages for friends and relatives. The result was that a high proportion of immigrants—estimated between 40 and 65 per cent in 1901—traveled on prepaid tickets or paid their fares with remittances received from the United States.

But although the development of the modern steamship network did much to "grease the wheels of emigration," the essential forces underlying the movement lay, as in earlier periods, in the widening impact of economic change. When in 1886 the State Department called upon American consuls in different parts of Europe to report on the extent and character of the exodus, virtually all of them told the same story. They agreed on the predominance of the economic motive and on the fact that all over Europe a similar set of economic pressures was at work. Local conditions and catastrophes could provide an added incentive to emigrate: a famine in Sweden, a blight on the vineyards in Croatia and Carniola, the creation of a French protective wall against Italian wines, the collapse of the market for Greek currants. But the main impetus to emigration came from more universal influences—the pressure of mounting population and the collapse of an age-old economic order. In the last quarter of the nineteenth century, country after country was hit by the kind of agrarian crisis that had afflicted Ireland and southwest Germany a generation earlier. In England, Sweden, and Germany east of the Elbe a catastrophic agricultural depression was brought on in the 1880s by the competition of cheap wheat from the United States, Canada, and Argentina. In the Austro-Hungarian Empire and in Russia the abolition of feudal dues and the emancipation of the serfs broke up the old system of landholding. Once they were permitted to subdivide their land the peasants did so on such a scale that the tiny holdings could no longer support those who lived on them. In Italy the agricultural situation got steadily worse, especially in the overcrowded, infertile, and poverty-stricken south, which groaned under an unjust land system reminiscent of pre-famine Ireland and where absentee landlordism and excessive subdivision of holdings produced their usual grim effects.

It should be remembered, however, that not all the peasants and agricultural laborers uprooted by these changes left Europe. Many flocked to the expanding industrial cities in their own or neighboring countries. That was how Germany came by its large Polish minority and France its Italian and Spanish population. Nor, when

Europeans sought new homes overseas, was the United States the only magnet. A substantial proportion of the British and Irish—indeed the majority after 1900—chose to settle in Canada or Australia; the Italians and Portuguese for a long time preferred South America. Nevertheless no other country had so large or so varied an immigrant influx as the United States.

The economic motive for emigration was never exclusive. Political and religious pressures also had an expulsive effect. Many young men, especially in Germany, Austria-Hungary, and Italy, emigrated in order to escape compulsory military service. Considerable numbers of Russian Jews fled their native land to escape the persecution and repression initiated by the Czarist government in 1881. But it would be an oversimplification to attribute the huge Jewish exodus from eastern Europe solely to the severity of Czarist policies, or even to the frightful pogroms that occurred periodically in Russia and Rumania. The worsening situation of east European Jewry was largely the product of the same economic factors that operated elsewhere—the rise in population and the narrowing of economic opportunity resulting from the collapse of the old agricultural order. In any case Jewish emigration from Russia was well under way before persecution became widespread or systematic, and there was just as heavy a Jewish emigration from areas such as Austrian Galicia where there was no persecution. Czarist repression could not, therefore, have been the major reason for Jewish emigration. Nevertheless, coming on top of a deteriorating economic situation—and indeed contributing to it—it helped convince countless Jews that there was no future for them in Russia.

Changing Conditions of Passage

In one respect those who emigrated to America after 1870 or so had an easier time than their predecessors. The transition from sail to steam, which was complete within a decade of the end of the Civil War, robbed the Atlantic crossing of its worst terrors. The journey by sail had taken anything between one and three months, but steamships took only ten days to reach New York from Liverpool or Bremen, and only fourteen days from Naples. Partly because of the reduction in the time of passage, partly because of advances in disease control, sickness and mortality on immigrant ships dropped sharply. The cholera outbreak on a group of National Line steamers in

"Many older persons among us," wrote one Italian immigrant, ". . . had been openly weeping ever since we entered the final approach to the unknown."
Right: Immigrants wait to disembark in New York.

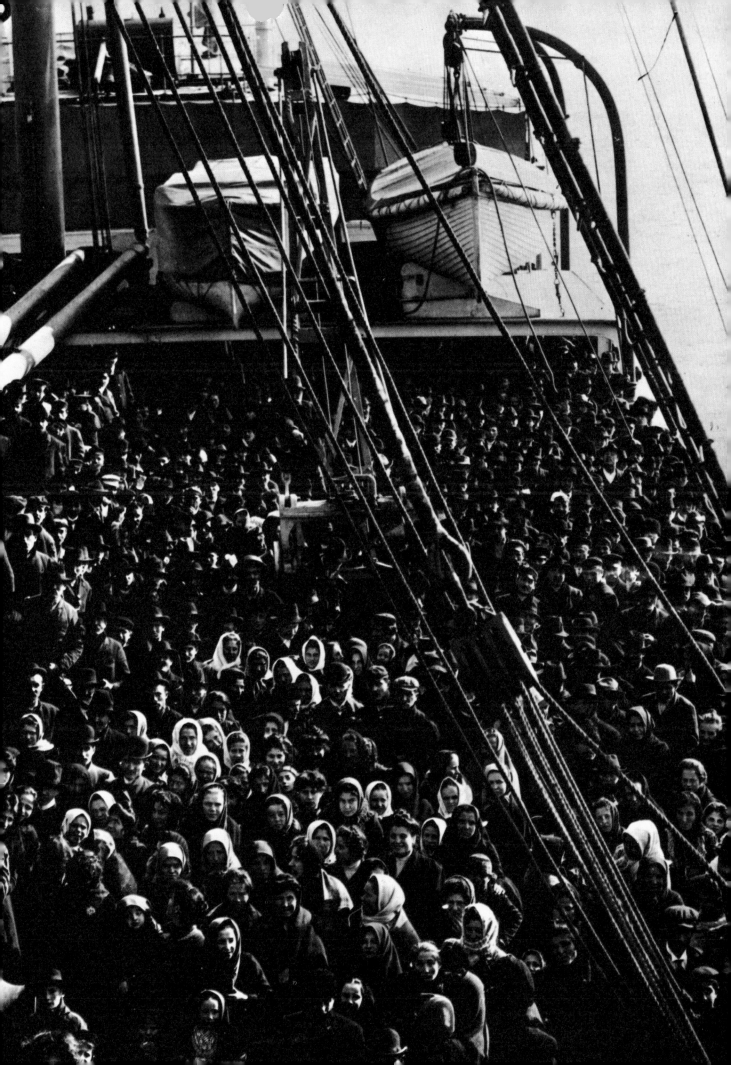

1866 was the last of its kind, though typhus and smallpox continued to break out occasionally even in the 1890s. But if the "horrors of the steerage" were now a thing of the past, conditions during the crossing still left much to be desired. Even on the huge new liners the steerage could be a crowded and unwholesome place. The passengers had to eat and sleep in the same compartment; privacy was impossible and cleanliness difficult to maintain, especially in rough weather when access to the deck was restricted. Food, though plentiful, was often badly prepared and washing facilities tended to be dirty and inadequate. Moreover, neglect and abuse of the passengers by the crew were still commonplace. Especially frequent were attacks on the chastity of unaccompanied females. To sympathetic observers what made such conditions more reprehensible was that they existed side by side with ornate luxury. It was the steerage which subsidized the banquets, the chandeliers, the palm courts, and the swimming pools enjoyed by the cabin passengers.

Public indignation about the squalid state in which immigrant ships still arrived from time to time led to demands for stronger action by Congress. But the revised Passenger Act which came into effect in 1882 made little difference. Enforcement machinery was inadequate and when prosecutions were begun for overcrowding or other infringements of the law, conviction was difficult because the immigrant witnesses had dispersed to their destinations. A study of the problem in 1873 by Treasury officials revealed what had been long evident—that the only effective method of regulating steerage conditions was by international agreement. But an American proposal for an immigrant ship convention was rejected by European governments; they were not willing to place their ships under the jurisdiction of American courts.

The Atlantic crossing over, immigrants might well have felt uplifted as they entered New York Harbor and gazed for the first time at the Statue of Liberty, symbol of America's welcome to the oppressed. But optimism must have been tempered with apprehension at the thought of the ordeal that awaited them at Ellis Island. From 1892 onward, when it replaced Castle Garden as New York's immigrant landing depot, Ellis Island served as a gigantic sieve, so designed as to exclude various categories of undesirables. Those found to have infectious diseases were sent back to Europe. So were unaccompanied women who were believed to be or suspected of being pregnant. The same fate awaited prostitutes, anarchists, convicts, and polygamists—provided, of course, that the immigration inspectors succeeded in detecting them. Nor was it easy to satisfy the authorities as to one's capacity to earn a living. If an immigrant arrived without any visible means of support, he ran the risk of being deported as a potential public charge. Yet if he admitted that he had a specific job to go to, he could be excluded under the contract labor law. Small wonder that immigrants should

Charles Ulrich's sympathetic painting In the Land of Promise (1884) focuses on new immigrants who sit in the bleak waiting room at Castle Garden. The landing depot was moved to Ellis Island in 1892.

have felt that the day of their arrival at New York was, as one of them put it, "the nearest earthly likeness to the final Day of Judgment, when we have to prove our fitness to enter Heaven." From early in the morning to late in the afternoon newcomers were driven in herds from one place to another; ranged into files; passed in review before doctors; poked, prodded, and quizzed by a succession of officials. Only when they had successfully run these multiple gauntlets were they allowed to catch the ferry to Manhattan. Here, tagged and ticketed like so many pieces of freight, and clutching their pathetic bundles of clothing, they at last set foot on the promised land.

Settlement and Employment Patterns

One of the strongest characteristics of the new immigration was a tendency among newcomers to congregate in the industrial cities of the Northeast. This was less of a novelty than contemporaries liked to think. The Irish half a century earlier had shown a marked proclivity for urban life, and so too had a fair proportion of the Germans, the British, and the Swedes. All the same there is no disputing the fact that new immigrants almost invariably became city dwellers. Agriculture had little appeal for them. They lacked the capital to begin farming and they were attracted by the high wages they could get in factories, mines, and mills. Thus only a tiny minority were to be found on the land.

This preference for urban life gave American cities a strongly foreign flavor. By 1910 one-third of the population of the twelve large cities was foreign-born and another third was made up of the children of immigrants. New York had more Italians than Naples, more Germans than Hamburg, and twice as many Irish as Dublin; Chicago boasted more Poles than Warsaw, more Czechs than Prague. Nor was cosmopolitanism confined to the largest cities. Smaller places like Oshkosh, Wisconsin; Lowell, Massachusetts; and Passaic, New Jersey, had just as large a proportion of foreign-born inhabitants.

Yet among the various immigrant groups there were important differences in distribution. This arose out of the tendency for each group to concentrate in particular industries—Russian and Polish Jews in the garment trade; Poles, Slovaks, and Lithuanians in mining and heavy industry; Italians in construction work; and from

When they arrived at New York, the newcomers were sent to the Immigrant Building at Ellis Island. There each underwent a physical and mental examination, as well as interrogation by the authorities. This 1904 photograph conveys the massive scale of the operation. Inset: A young woman has her physical.

across the border, French Canadians in textiles. But no matter what the job was, the immigrant experience was generally one of long hours, exploitation, and insanitary and dangerous conditions of work. These evils were, perhaps, most notorious in the ready-made clothing industry. Under the sweating system which characterized the garment trade men, women, and children toiled for as much as sixteen hours a day either in steam-filled, poorly lit sweatshops or in the squalid tenements in which they made their homes.

Conditions in mines and factories were, if anything, even worse. Wages were high, but the pace was killing and the accident rate staggering. Employers in the mining industry were apt to attribute the frequency of accidents to the recklessness, ignorance, and inexperience of the immigrants themselves, especially those from southern and eastern Europe. But if the fault lay with the immigrant, it was difficult to understand why the accident rate in American mines was so much higher than in, say, Russia or Austria-Hungary. A more probable explanation of the difference lay in the absence of adequate supervision of inexperienced employees in American mines and a flagrant disregard of elementary safety precautions.

The problem of child labor, which attracted increasing public attention around the turn of the century, was not wholly created by immigration: it was widespread in the South, which had few immigrants. But it was immigrant children who suffered most. Jewish and Italian children were extensively employed in the garment industry; children of French-Canadian parentage were prominent in the textile mills of New England; Slavic, Hungarian, and Italian "breaker boys" played an important role in the Pennsylvania anthracite mines. Every state had child labor laws on the statute book, but they proved difficult to enforce—not least because of the resistance and evasion of parents, for whom the earnings of their offspring were a vital element in the family budget.

Exploitation of a different kind characterized Italian immigration. The culprit was the padrone or work-boss. He was a labor agent, usually of Italian origin, who supplied American employers, especially in the construction industry, with gangs of workmen at prearranged rates. Newly arrived Italians, unfamiliar with American conditions and unable to speak English, found the padrone's help invaluable. He found them work, transported them to their place of employment, and provided them with food and lodging. But the accommodation provided for Italian track gangs was extremely primitive. Usually the men slept in dilapidated railroad cars or in shanty bunk houses roughly constructed of corrugated iron. They were compelled to pay extortionate prices to the padrone for food and other necessities. At its worst the padrone system was almost the equivalent of peonage.

By the end of the nineteenth century, immigrants formed the mass of the wage earners in every major

*Work-hungry and unskilled, immigrants were frequently
concentrated in the nation's lowest-paid jobs. Here are three
representative occupations. Top: Workers on the New York
State Barge Canal relax in their bunkhouse. Right: At the
turn of the century, mine owners thought nothing of sending
young boys down to work in the pits. Above: In crowded
and unhealthy conditions, New York garment workers
toil in a "sweatshop."*

industry—steel, coal mining, textiles, clothing manufacture, slaughtering, and meat packing. In each of these industries, the shift in the sources of immigration had produced striking changes in the composition of the labor force. Everywhere the new immigrants were coming to predominate. In bituminous coal mining Slovaks, Poles, Hungarians, and Italians took the place of native-born Americans and British, Irish, and German immigrants; in New England textile factories Greeks, Portuguese, French-Canadians, Poles, Italians, and Syrians gradually supplanted Irish and English operatives. What made the change of personnel possible was the increased use of machinery: the adoption of mechanical devices and processes enabled American industry to absorb large numbers of unskilled and inexperienced newcomers.

Contemporaries often viewed these developments unfavorably. They complained of native-born Americans and older immigrants having been "displaced"—in the sense of having been forced out by immigrants with lower standards of living and a readiness to accept subsistence wages. Whether this is what actually happened in American industry to any considerable extent is highly doubtful. The new immigration does not appear to have had any general long-term effect on wage rates, nor to have caused serious unemployment. Some of the workers said to have been displaced moved up, in fact, to supervisory and managerial jobs; others voluntarily sought fresh employment because they were unwilling to work with newcomers whose habits they found uncongenial and whom they despised as "Hunkies" or "Dagoes." This is not to say that certain groups of craftsmen did not feel the pinch of immigrant competition: tailors, carpenters, housepainters, and shoemakers were among those who did, though it is unclear how far their difficulties were caused by immigration and how far by mechanization. But most groups of workers seem to have had few complaints. In 1898 the New York State Bureau of Labor Statistics called upon every labor organization in the state to report whether their members had been directly and detrimentally affected by immigrant labor and whether wage rates had been reduced by immigrant competition. Three-quarters of the replies received were negative.

A related and more widespread complaint was that new immigrants were reluctant to join trade unions and, because of their docility and language difficulties, hindered the unionization of occupations and industries in which they were engaged. It is easy to see why labor leaders should have looked askance at the new immigration. In the 1870s and 1880s Slavic, Hungarian, and Italian immigrants were frequently used as strikebreakers, especially in the Pennsylvania coal fields. Moreover it was perfectly true that relatively few of the new immigrants belonged to trade unions, even when they had been in the United States for some years. But this was hardly surprising given that the new immigrants were largely unskilled and that most unions catered only for craft workers.

In any case few serious efforts were made to organize newcomers from southern and eastern Europe. When they were, the response was remarkable. Thus in the Pennsylvania anthracite coal fields, John Mitchell's success in recruiting Slavic miners for the United Mine Workers in the 1890s was a major reason for the success of the anthracite coal strike of 1902. Poles, Lithuanians, Slovaks, and Ukrainians forgot their mutual animosities and to a man responded to the strike call. An even more impressive instance of immigrant participation in labor unions was provided by the garment industry. Despite the fact that three-quarters of the employees were foreign-born—mainly Jews, Italians, Czechs, and Poles—the Amalgamated Clothing Workers of America and the International Ladies' Garment Workers' Union were by 1914 among the strongest labor unions in the country. What is more, they were very largely immigrant creations.

Life in the Ghettos

Despite such instances of ethnic collaboration, immigrants did not mix to any great extent with people of different origin. Rather they would cling to their own kind. Each group tended to occupy a distinct residential neighborhood and to move elsewhere whenever strangers began to appear. A plan of ethnic neighborhoods thus resembled a mosaic. But although ethnic ghettos bore such names as "Little Italy" or *Kleindeutschland,* the use of such labels was misleading. In fact, immigrants clustered in provincial rather than in national groups. For example, the Italian population of New York did not live together indiscriminately: Neapolitans, Sicilians, Lombardians, and Piedmontese each had exclusive possession of particular streets.

Forced by their poverty to take the cheapest accommodations they could find, newcomers occupied some of the worst slums to be found anywhere in the world. Every large American city had its teeming and congested immigrant districts; but New York's Lower East Side, with its huge concentrations of Irish, Germans, Jews, Italians, and others provided the most conspicuous and notorious example. Jacob Riis, the Danish-born journalist and reformer, produced a classic indictment of New York slum life in his newspaper articles, published in book form as *How the Other Half Lives* in 1890. He described for instance the maze of filthy, stinking courts and back alleys

Inhabited mostly by Italians, Mulberry Street was just one of New York's immigrant slums. The squalid conditions which prevailed are very much in evidence in this 1889 photograph of "Bandit's Roost."

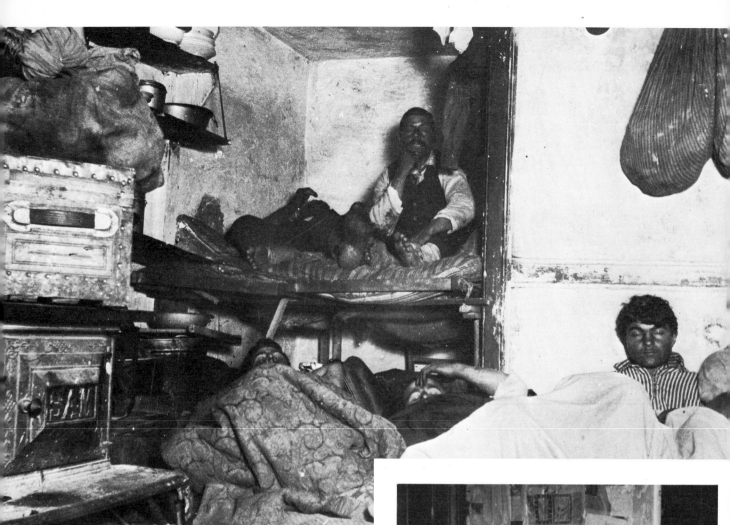

The conditions of immigrant life shocked those few Americans who studied them. For this "spot" (temporary) dwelling, the Italian family shown paid about five cents a night each. Jacob Riis took the photograph. Right: Posing inside their tenement, these two women have not found America "the golden door."

of Mulberry Bend, occupied mainly by Italians. Here were to be found the worst examples of overcrowding and the highest death rates in the city. "There is but one 'Bend' in the world," wrote Riis, "and that is enough." But conditions were hardly any better in nearby Hester Street, at the heart of the Jewish quarter. Contemporary journalists like Riis were fascinated by the color and vibrancy of the Jewish Lower East Side and later writers —especially those who, having been born in the ghetto, escaped from it—have painted an affectionate and romanticized picture. The Jewish Lower East Side did indeed possess a warmth, a picturesqueness, and a rich intellectual life—in short, a special quality that author Hutchins Hapgood was to call "the spirit of the ghetto." But however great the inner compensation the external reality was harsh. Each of the "dumbbell" tenements—

grim, insanitary, six-story firetraps, honeycombed with dark, tiny rooms—was the home of scores of families.

But if the cities had the worst black spots, housing conditions could be just as frightful in mining and industrial areas. The novelist Frank Norris, visiting the Pennsylvania anthracite regions during the strike of 1902, was appalled by what he saw. He described how, at the town of Melonsville, he found groups of Polish miners occupying tiny hovels not fit for dogs and shuddered at the thought that human beings lived thus. Norris carried away from Melonsville memories only of "its meanness, its grime, its rain, its grayness and blackness and sordidness, its foul sweet stench and huddled hutches, its hideous promiscuousness and execrable, maddening dreariness." He found himself wondering why its miners were content merely with striking.

Native Americans like Norris who were prepared to take the trouble can have had little difficulty in seeing just how grim were the physical conditions under which immigrants lived. But only the immigrants themselves can have comprehended the magnitude of the adjustment they had been called upon to make in coming to America. Immigration had brought about an abrupt break in their lives. They had cut themselves off from a familiar environment and faced the need to come to terms with an unpredictable, confusing one. Little wonder that immigration could have traumatic effects; that simple, ignorant folk from European villages and towns should have felt bewildered, overwhelmed even, by their first contact with the hurly-burly of the American city. Such were the feelings that inspired a literature of immigration —novels like Abraham Cahan's *The Rise of David Levinsky* and Ole E. Rolvaag's *Giants in the Earth*. Works such as these were written out of the novelists' own experiences; they provide glimpses of the psychological impact of immigration upon those who took part in it.

Of all the trials incident to immigration one of the most keenly felt was the disruption of family life. Separation was often implicit in migration, since lack of money made it difficult for the whole family to go at the same time. The usual practice was for the husband to go on ahead and to send for his wife and family as soon as he had earned enough to pay for their passages. That was why so many immigrants accepted low living standards during their first years in America. Sometimes the family was reunited within months; often it took much longer. The period of separation, especially if protracted, placed family relationships under stress. Letters came slowly and were an inadequate means of expression for uneducated peasants; as time went on letters tended to arrive less regularly and sometimes to cease altogether. The frequency with which families were fragmented by immigration was suggested by the regularity with which advertisements appeared in the immigrant press asking for information about relatives with whom contact had been lost.

Cultural Transitions

It was perhaps inevitable that family disorganization should have been common. In the old country marriage ties had been regarded as indissoluble, but under American conditions they tended to loosen. Separation often led one partner or both to enter into irregular sexual liaisons. Moreover the imbalance in the sex ratio and the practice of taking lodgers into the family home sometimes tempted immigrant wives to desert their husbands. There were other reasons too why marital obligations were more readily cast off in America. Immigrants came to a country in which there was much more sexual equality than in Europe and in which the possibility of divorce existed. In addition, the social restraints that had existed in Europe in the form of the church and of a homogeneous public opinion were weakened or removed. With the breakdown of these restraints, immigrant marriages often proved difficult to sustain.

Immigration tended also to create a gulf between parents and children. Parental control on the strict European model proved impossible in America because the social and legal sanctions needed to maintain it were lacking. There was thus an erosion of traditional patterns of authority, obedience, and respect. More shattering still was the fact that the normal relationship between parent and child had been reversed by the conditions of immigrant life. Immigrant children, exposed to the influences of the school, became Americanized much more rapidly than their parents. That circumstance gave children a practical superiority over their elders when it came to adjusting to the strange new American world. Indeed, in their anxiety to be accepted as Americans immigrant children often rejected their old world heritage and sometimes the parents who symbolized it. It was not unusual for parents to find that within the family circle their values were belittled, their loyalties scorned, their speech and appearance ridiculed. The painful tensions which arose in consequence led parents to complain bitterly of the rebelliousness and indiscipline of youth. At the same time the breakdown of parental authority was a major reason for the prevalence of delinquency among the second generation.

The disorganizing nature of their experiences in the New World and the hostility they often encountered at the hands of the native-born stimulated in immigrants an awareness of their own identity and a deep desire for emotional security in the company of their own kind. That was why each group congregated in distinctive neighborhoods and why they established their own social institutions—churches, schools, newspapers, and mutual aid societies.

The generalization that religion was the focal point of immigrant life was truer of some groups than of others. Some of the newcomers—the Irish and the Poles are the best examples—displayed a fervent devotion to their faith. Their chief aim in America was to reestablish the precise forms of the religious life they had known at home, and to achieve it they made tremendous personal sacrifices. It should be remembered, however, that church attendance was not necessarily a proof of religious conviction. The church was a social as well as a religious institution, and the weekly church service could be welcomed also as an opportunity to greet and mix with old friends. Not infrequently, however, separation from the religious environment in which they had been reared led to a loss of faith or at least to the severance of all connection with the ancestral church. This so-called leakage was associated particularly with Italians who, according to the Catholic clergy, were casual in attending Mass and largely indifferent to the doctrines of the church. Italians nonetheless were assiduous in observing church holidays and saints' days—or at least in joining in the public festivities which marked such occasions. The popularity of the Italian festa was, of course, primarily due to religious devotion, but while it was in form a religious observance it was also a secular holiday characterized by a good deal of gaiety. After the religious procession was over the bands played rousing tunes, pizza-sellers did a roaring trade, and the day generally ended with a firework display.

The significance of foreign-language newspapers is suggested by their number—there were more than 2,000 of them when they reached their heyday just before the First World War. Their popularity was not difficult to explain, for they reflected and expressed in familiar terms the attitudes and aspirations of their readers. This was especially true of that most celebrated of immigrant newspapers, the *Jewish Daily Forward,* published in Yiddish. The *Forward*'s best-known feature was the *bintl brief*—literally a bundle of letters—which was in effect an advice column dealing with everyday problems of immigrant life. But the paper was also a mine of information about group activities and the American social and political scene. Its principal function was to help the immigrant adjust by introducing him to American life. Nativists sometimes looked disapprovingly at the growth of a foreign-language press which appeared to them to retard Americanization. But in content and style immigrant newspapers were characteristically American; their distinctiveness consisted mainly in the fact that they were published in a language other than English.

Of the numerous cultural institutions that flourished in immigrant communities none was better adapted to the understanding and tastes of newcomers than the theater. Immigrant audiences were rarely cultivated or sophisticated and most of them lacked any previous acquain-

Patterned after churches in the "old country," the immigrant churches in America provided ethnic continuity. A predominantly Norwegian congregation poses outside its church in Blue Mounds, Wisconsin.

tance with the stage. To appeal to such people plots had to be simple, character sharply drawn, and the action had to consist either of broad comedy or of a succession of sensational incidents and violent appeals to the emotions. Invariably, too, there had to be a happy ending. Farce and melodrama were thus the staple offerings of the immigrant theaters developed by the Germans, Swedes, Italians, Poles, and Jews. The Yiddish theater, however, outshone all the rest; it was beyond question the most effective vehicle of popular culture among Lower East Side Jews.

The hazards and uncertainties of immigrant life suggested the need for some form of mutual aid society.

Typically a society would come into being when a group of individuals began to turn over to one of their number, or to a boardinghouse keeper, a proportion of their earnings for use in sickness, accident, or other emergency. Out of this practice developed a wide range of autonomous organizations to care for the needy and protect the helpless. At first such societies were organized on a local or regional basis, but in time they federated along the lines of nationality and assumed such names as the Order of Sons of Italy, the Polish National Alliance, and the Pan Hellenic Union. In the course of time such bodies came to have larger aims than the mere provision of insurance benefits, endowing educational and civic programs.

For all the emphasis they placed on mutual self-help, immigrants discovered that they did not have to rely solely on themselves in their efforts to adjust to America. Since they were entitled to vote within a short time of their arrival, they could call upon ward politicians for help and protection. Political machines coveted the immigrant's vote and for the sake of controlling it were prepared to become his benefactor. On the eve of the First World War a leading Progressive, Edward A. Ross, outlined the services provided:

It is Alderman Tim who gets the Italian a permit for his push-cart or fruit-stand, who finds him a city-hall job, who protects him if he violates law or ordinance in running his business, who goes his bail if he is arrested and 'fixes things' with the police judge or the state's attorney when he comes to trial. Even before Giuseppe is naturalized it is Tim who remembers him at Christmas with a big turkey, pays his rent at a pinch, or wins his undying gratitude by saving his baby from a pauper burial or sending carriages and flowers to the funeral.

Reformers like Ross complained bitterly that immigrant support of corrupt machines frustrated their attempts to purify politics. But the average immigrant had no comprehension of the reformer's concept that politics was a field for disinterested public service. Beset by pressing personal needs, the newcomer was incapable of responding to appeals to civic virtue. He supported instead those who were prepared to do something for him.

Nativist Hostility Increases

The feeling that ignorant immigrants were debasing American politics was one reason for the growth of nativist hostility in the closing decades of the nineteenth century. Another was the fear of immigrant radicalism, about which alarm became widespread after the Haymarket bomb outrage in Chicago in 1886. The conviction of a group of foreign-born anarchists for the crime encouraged Americans to think of immigrants generally as violent revolutionaries. It should have been evident that the vast majority of immigrants was not interested in revolution, but the stereotype of the long-haired, wild-eyed foreign radical persisted—indeed was apparently confirmed in 1901 when President McKinley was assassinated by an anarchist named Leon Czolgosz.

While immigrants in general were associated in the popular mind with lawlessness, a special stigma attached to Italians, especially those from southern Italy and Sicily. They were believed to have innately violent inclinations, a notion which derived some support from the high incidence of stabbings and shootings in Italian neighborhoods. When these were followed by a wave of bombings and murders among New York's Italians, the image was conjured up of a mysterious criminal organization—the Mafia or the Black Hand—whose activities were believed to extend from Italy to every sizable American city. Such ideas brought on a violent anti-Italian reaction in the 1890s. In several parts of the South and the West, Italians charged with crime were summarily executed by native-born vigilantes. The best-known incident occurred at New Orleans in 1890. After a jury had failed to convict a group of Italians accused of the murder of the city's police chief, an infuriated mob broke into the parish prison and lynched them.

Another source of nativist concern was the fact that under the impact of immigration the United States was losing its original Protestant character. The predominantly Catholic coloring of the influx after 1880, the spectacular expansion of the Catholic parochial school system, and the growing prominence in American cities of Irish Catholic politicians contributed to a revival of popular anti-Catholicism. The American Protective Association came into being in 1886 with the aim of limiting Catholic political power and of defending the public school system against what was seen as a papal attack. The APA whipped up anti-Catholic hysteria with wild talk of a threatened papal conquest of the United States and attracted a good deal of support, especially in rural areas of the Middle West. And although the APA fizzled out in the mid-1890s, anti-Catholicism continued to simmer below the surface.

Simultaneously there were increasing manifestations of hostility toward Jews. This took a variety of forms. It could erupt in physical assault on individual Jews or in anti-Jewish riots; it could produce vicious racist slurs and crude caricatures of Jews in the popular press. But a more characteristic expression of anti-Semitism was social and economic discrimination. From the late 1880s, Jews found themselves increasingly excluded from clubs, hotels, summer resorts, and private schools; restrictive covenants barred them from living in certain areas; obstacles were placed in their path when they sought to enter white-collar occupations. These restrictions were due partly to resentment at the speed with which Jews advanced socially and economically. But what gave added force to anti-Semitism was fear of Jewish financial power. Ignatius Donnelly's popular novel of the future, *Caesar's Column,* was the best known of several expressions of this fear.

It would be wrong, however, to give the impression that the late-nineteenth-century nativist revival was wholly the product of prejudice and irrational fear. Many Americans were honestly worried about foreign influences because they doubted the nation's capacity to absorb such huge numbers of immigrants. They particularly wondered whether newcomers whose cultural and economic backgrounds were so different from their own could ever be Americanized. They were concerned lest newcomers from southern and eastern Europe remain an indigestible lump, hindering the development of national unity and, because of their rate of increase, threatening to swamp what was thought of as "the native American stock." Thus the immigration restriction movement, which developed out of the anxieties of the 1880s, did not aim at an end to immigration; it sought rather to exclude only those newcomers regarded as inferior and unassimilable—in short, the new immigrants.

The Immigrant Flood Subsides

The demand for a selective immigration policy derived much of its support from labor unions. In their campaign against contract labor, which they persuaded Congress to outlaw in 1886, the Knights of Labor directed their fire against immigrants from southern and eastern Europe whom they mistakenly believed to be contract

To honor America's centennial of independence, France presented to the United States the Statue of Liberty. Great jubilation marked the unveiling, which took place in 1886—in a downpour.

LOOKING BACKWARD.
They would close to the New Comer the Bridge that Carried Them and their Fathers Over.

Not only native-born Americans harbored anti-immigrant feelings. Against the silhouettes of their former selves, these immigrants-turned-bigshots reject the Europeans who now follow in their path.

laborers and whose low living standards they saw as a threat to the American workingman. This attitude was inherited by the American Federation of Labor, whose president Samuel Gompers became an outspoken restrictionist despite his own immigrant background. But the spearhead of the restrictionist movement and its main ideological driving force was the Immigration Restriction League, founded in 1894 by a group of race-conscious Boston aristocrats. It was the league which popularized the notion that the new immigration was a collective entity, different from and inferior to the old. Arguing that the "Anglo-Saxon" element in the American population was in danger of being engulfed by lesser breeds, the league campaigned energetically for an immigration policy which would exclude those allegedly inferior groups while continuing to admit those to which, it was claimed, America owed her greatness. To achieve this end they advocated not the exclusion of particular ethnic groups—overt discrimination they were anxious to avoid—but the application of a literacy test.

Concerned though Americans were about immigration, not all of them were persuaded by the league's arguments. Many continued to believe that the disadvantages of birth could be made to yield to the influence of the American environment. Still more were reluctant to repudiate the asylum ideal which had inspired Emma Lazarus's poem, inscribed on the base of the Statue of Liberty:

Give me your tired, your poor,

Your huddled masses yearning to breathe free,

The wretched refuse of your teeming shore.

Send these, the homeless, tempest-tost to me.

I lift my lamp beside the golden door.

Even those who accepted the need for some kind of restriction had misgivings about the literacy test; they felt it was a test, not of ability, but of opportunity. That was why literacy test bills were vetoed successively by Presidents Cleveland, Taft, and Wilson. Only after twenty years of agitation was the literacy test enacted into law over another Wilsonian veto; its passage in 1917 was the result of the nationalist fervor created by the First World War. The literacy test did not in fact do much to exclude southern and eastern Europeans; when the ability to read was made as the test of entry, "new" immigrants acquired it almost overnight. But the quota laws of 1921 and 1924 effectively shut the gates to them as well as bringing about a drastic reduction in immigration generally.

The United States was not, of course, alone in restricting immigration in the early twentieth century: Canada, Australia, Argentina, and Brazil all did the same. In fact all the nations of the world were now putting up bars against strangers. The era of free movement of peoples was drawing to a close; that of passports, visas, quotas, and restrictions was beginning. Yet however much restriction was a universal phenomenon, it had special implications for America. A huge folk-migration that had gone on for three centuries was brought summarily to an end. A long-standing tradition of asylum had been repudiated and with it the cosmopolitan ideal of nationality.

Labor on the Move

The beckoning jaws of American industry clamped shut on millions of workers from the countryside and from abroad in the decades following the Civil War. As these men and women discovered what factory life was really like, they came to feel that they should be compensated by a greater share of the wealth they helped to produce. The workers therefore developed by the 1890s a potent form of labor unionism. The objective of most labor unionists by the 1890s was neither revolution nor reform. They were concerned simply to wrest concessions from the employers in their own trades. The triumph of this relatively conservative outlook was the result of a century of experience, and particularly of the intensified activity of the period since the 1860s.

In the 1860s American wage earners had found themselves under the spell of a great innovator from Philadelphia, William H. Sylvis. Through the example of the Iron Molders' International Union, of which he was the founder and leader, Sylvis introduced the idea of a "national" union (called "international" in order to embrace Canada). His union would outlaw unofficial work stoppages and concentrate its carefully guarded central funds in order to finance a few, strategically chosen, strikes. In 1864 Sylvis described the initial effect that such a policy had on his own union: "From a mere pigmy, our union has in one short year grown to be a giant." Shortly afterward, a combination of employers, assisted by the demoralizing effect of an industrial recession, weakened the Iron Molders' International Union and persuaded Sylvis to broaden his approach to labor organization.

In trying to strengthen the American labor movement as a whole, Sylvis showed himself to be an idealist. Wearing the same threadbare clothes, he traveled throughout the United States and Canada in a determined effort to organize new unions until he died in poverty in 1869. He expected a similar self-denial of other labor unionists. In 1867 he persuaded the newly established National Labor Union to adopt a reform program designed to help not only American labor organizations, but also Negroes, women in search of emancipation, consumers, and even the wage earners of Europe. Those labor leaders who had met to form the NLU in 1866 found they could not unite behind such policies. Many of them had supported the NLU with a specific reform in mind. Ira Steward of Boston, for example, became known as the "eight hour monomaniac" because of his reputed inability to see further than the need for a shorter working day. When Sylvis died, support for the NLU crumbled.

Of all Sylvis's ideas, that of organizing labor unions on national lines proved the most enduring. The way in which a national union could collect membership dues all over the country and conserve them in a central treasury allowed for survival in the face of the worst depressions. The Panic of 1873, however, tested the very best of organizations. It followed on the failure of the banking house of Jay Cooke and Company, which caused hysteria in the business community and triggered about 5,000 further commercial failures in the fall of 1873. Lack of confidence among the capitalists led to a decline in industrial activity and a rise in unemployment. By 1877 only one-fifth of the workers had steady jobs, and about 3 million could find no employment whatsoever. Great suffering was inevitable; in New York City 90,000 people, two-fifths of them women, had been evicted from their homes by the spring of 1874 because of their inability to pay rent.

Because of their desperate situation, men had to take jobs under any conditions. In the New York building trades, wages of $1.50–$2.50 for a ten-hour day replaced the former rates of $2.50–$3.00 for eight hours' work. The bargaining power of labor unionists declined; employers no longer had to accept union rates and hire union members. By 1878 there were only 50,000 union members compared with 300,000 five years earlier. Of the thirty national labor unions in existence in 1873, only eight survived the depression.

But the attention of most Americans was riveted in the 1870s on the violent response of a minority of workers to the problems of the depression. Labor violence erupted with an intensity never matched before or since in American history. The most notorious episode was the murder of a number of Welsh and English Protestants who opposed the militant strike tactics of Pennsylvania miners. Mine owners attributed these killings to Catholic militants allegedly organized into a secret society named after the "matchless Molly Maguire," who had resisted British rule in Ireland. These owners hired a Pinkerton detective, James McParlan, to infiltrate and obtain information against the murderers in the coal fields. A "cold soak" who could drink anyone under the table—and in the process extract drunken indiscretions—McParlan was responsible for the trial, conviction, and hanging of several Pennsylvania labor leaders on charges of association with the "Mollies."

The labor press protested that defense witnesses had been intimidated during the "Molly Maguire" trials. The papers also said that McParlan had actually provoked atrocities where miners intended none, pinning responsibility on militants whom the English and Welsh bosses wanted out of the way. The most that can be proved against McParlan is that he did not warn those whom he knew were earmarked for liquidation. Whether or not the accusations against McParlan were true, by 1877 the American public was beginning to take notice of the allegations of injustice expressed by laboring men.

In that year, a strike on the Baltimore & Ohio Rail-

The Great Strike of 1877 started in West Virginia,
but soon spread quickly to other states. Above:
Vandalized property of the Pennsylvania Railroad.

road spread throughout the nation, resulting in serious rioting and destruction of property in Pittsburgh and Chicago. Troops deployed against the rioters opened fire, and there were scores of casualties. In some cases, however, the soldiers refused to shoot, because, as one New York officer protested, "We may be militiamen, but we are workmen first." Because of their well-known reputation for corruption, railroads were unpopular among small businessmen and farmers, as well as among workingmen. After 1877 it was no longer safe to assume that public opinion would automatically support employers against strikers.

The prospect of gaining support for their cause from the American public induced large numbers of workers to turn to a leader who believed that reform could be achieved through education. They found their man in Terence V. Powderly, an advocate of such reforms as the government ownership of public utilities and the abolition of child labor. He condemned strike action, supporting instead peaceful propaganda and the boycott of antiunion business.

In 1879 Powderly became grand master workman of the Knights of Labor, a minor labor organization characterized by secrecy and ritualistic ceremony. By 1885 membership of the organization had grown to 700,000. Several reasons accounted for the growth of the Knights under Powderly's leadership. Firstly, Powderly was

Under the leadership of Terence V. Powderly, the Knights of Labor enjoyed a reputation for moderate policies. Member craftsmen proudly displayed these cards bearing the picture of their leader.

successful in abolishing secrecy within the Knights; he thus gained the approval of the Catholic Church (which frowned upon clandestine ritual) and encouraged Catholic membership. Secondly, the subdivision of the Knights on geographical lines into district assemblies and their attack on monopoly capitalism attracted farmers and small businessmen into membership. Finally, recruitment was encouraged, to Powderly's disgust, by two successful strikes in 1885 against the Jay Gould railroad system.

By 1893, when Powderly was replaced as grand master workman, the Knights had diminished to 75,000 members. This decline was due partly to the resurgence of national unionism, partly to the failure of a third strike against the Gould system in 1886, and partly to other events tied to the great agitation of that year. Critics of Powderly upbraided him for withholding wholehearted support from the national strike in support of the eight-hour day which was planned for May 1. Powderly retorted that strikes only harmed the reputation of labor. He believed, however, that the crucial damage suffered by the Knights was a consequence not of the disputes of 1886, but of the Haymarket Bomb Affair.

The Haymarket Riot

Industrial tension in Chicago had been brewing in the spring of 1886 and it was predicted that on May 1 violence of some sort would take place. Thirty thousand men were on strike, but the day passed without incident. The forecast was off by three days. On the evening of May 4, workers assembled in Haymarket Square had their meeting foreshortened when someone within their crowd threw a bomb which killed a policeman. Thus began the Haymarket Riot.

The outbreak had its roots in another rally held the previous day outside the McCormick factory. August Spies, the speaker, addressed a crowd of 6,000 strikers, most of them from the Lumber Shovers' Union. Spies was sent from the Central Labor Union as a reporter, but he was asked by the Lumber Shovers to speak. He urged workers to band together until their demands were met. The Lumber Shovers were pressing for ten hours' pay for eight hours' work. Also present at the gathering were about 500 McCormick strikers, out over an internal dispute about unions.

Inside the factory nonstriking workers kept the plant functioning. The bell rang signifying the end of the day; when the workers filed out of the factory, they were attacked. McCormick strikers from the meeting pelted rocks and stones into their midst. Chasing them back into the factory, they broke several windows in the process.

Shots were fired—first by the plant police to disperse the violent mob and then by the strikers in response. Someone had called for help and no less than 200 police arrived on the scene. They met little resistance from the strikers and in a matter of minutes the incident was over. Yet one striker was killed, five or six seriously wounded, and several more injured to a lesser degree.

Spies saw May 3 as an act of police brutality. He called for a meeting to discuss the subject on the following evening, May 4. The place: Haymarket Square, on Randolph Street, between Desplaines and Halsted. Twenty thousand circulars were distributed beforehand and a crowd of at least that size was expected to turn up. Only between three and four thousand did, and more than a thousand people left because of impending bad weather.

Three radical speakers took their turns on the platform, each of them addressing the group on a particular aspect of the situation. The last speaker, Samuel Fielden, was just finishing his speech when a band of 180 police arrived.

"In the name of the people of the State of Illinois," warned Captain Ward, "I command this meeting immediately and peaceably to disperse." Fielden replied that they were a "peaceable" gathering. He was just descending the platform along with the other speakers when something quite unforeseen took place. A dynamite bomb shot up into the air and landed at the feet of the first rank of the policemen, killing one. The police promptly opened fire on the fleeing crowd. The whole melée lasted only a few seconds. One demonstrator was killed (another died later), and about seventy on both sides were injured. The press, both local and national, was filled with the incident for a good two weeks after the event.

Courtesy Chicago Historical Society

Led by the Chicago police, the hunt was on to find the bomb-thrower. Although they rounded up nearly 200 anarchists, the police did not find their man. Thirty-one men were charged with conspiracy to kill a police officer, and eight were convicted. One of the men was sentenced to fifteen years; the others to hang. Louis Lingg, a known manufacturer of bombs, blew himself up in his cell. In early November 1887 Spies and Fielden had their sentences commuted to life by the Illinois governor. The remaining four were executed on November 11 the same year.

The riot and subsequent executions inflamed public opinion on all sides. Many people believed that the strikers and rallies were part of an anarchist plot to overthrow the capitalist system. In that sense it was the first "red scare" in America. Unfortunately for the workers in search of better conditions, the affair "did more injury to the good name of labor than all the strikes that year. . . ." At least that was how Terence V. Powderly, grand master workman of the Knights of Labor, assessed the situation. Henry Demarest Lloyd saw the executions as a manifestation of fear: "They have been killed because property, authority, and public believed that they came to bring not reform but revolution, not peace but a sword. . . ."

August Spies (far left) organized the meeting in Haymarket Square at which three speakers urged worker solidarity. Just as the last was finishing his speech, the police arrived (below) to disperse the audience; minutes later the fateful bomb was thrown. Although the culprit was never found, eight men were found guilty of complicity. Left: Four of them await death on the gallows on November 11, 1887.

The Formation of the AFL

The incident in Haymarket Square caused a mood of anti-radical hysteria in the press and among the people. When the hysteria subsided, several Americans began to question the validity of the case against the eight convicted men. Dangerous though several of them may have been, there was little evidence to link them with the actual throwing of the Haymarket bomb. Indeed, only three of them had even been present at the ill-fated meeting. In 1893, Governor John P. Altgeld of Illinois pardoned the two survivors, who had in 1887 had their sentences commuted to life, and released them from jail.

Altgeld was to become a respected figure in the Democratic party, but in 1893 the Chicago *Tribune* voiced a widely held opinion saying that the German-born governor "was not merely an alien by birth, but an alien by temperament and sympathies." A substantial number of Americans held firm to the belief that the "martyrs" were murderers. Anarchism, and to some extent socialism, remained smeared with the brush of bloodshed. But the repercussions of the Haymarket explosion were not felt by radicals alone. Albert Parsons, one of the executed Haymarket speakers, was a member of the Knights of Labor. By preaching peaceful methods, the Knights had benefited from favorable public opinion after the riots of 1877. In 1886, as Powderly was the first to realize, their association with Parsons made them vulnerable to adverse opinion: this circumstance contributed to the disintegration of the Knights.

Whatever its effects on the Knights, the Haymarket affair failed to prevent the growth of the American Federation of Labor (AFL), a new organization formed in December 1886. The AFL was the fruition of three decades of experience since the death of Sylvis. Related to it were those national labor unions which, having survived the depression of the 1870s, were now gaining in strength. Leaders of these unions were formulating a new philosophy, based on the idea that a worker cared most of all about his own job, and was conscious only in a secondary way of the interest of the working class. AFL spokesmen argued that a worker could best improve the value of his job and himself by combining with others within his craft. Such banding together would ensure that they had an exclusive monopoly of the labor supply in their own trade. The AFL ideal was a "closed shop" of skilled craftsmen in every trade who could ensure good wages for their services, and whose constant demand was not for distant reforms

An amalgam of trade unions, the American Federation of Labor challenged the centralized structure espoused by the Knights of Labor. These union labels represent only a sample of the AFL's diversity.

to benefit all, but "more, more, now," for themselves.

The AFL membership increased each year between 1886 and 1892. There was a major economic depression in the mid-1890s, but this time the national unions weathered the storm. Membership in the AFL increased again after 1897 until it had reached 1.7 million out of a total 2 million union members by 1904. (Skilled railroad workers, organized into their own powerful "Brotherhoods," refused to affiliate with the AFL.) In 1886 the AFL had benefited at the expense of the Knights; its leaders had won respect by supporting the eight-hour movement; and the AFL itself, being formed in December, could be clearly dissociated from the violence of May. The national unions thereafter tightened up their finances and used their supreme weapon, the strike, with discrimination. They refused to support, for example, the general strike by unskilled railroad workers in 1894. When, however, the unskilled and semiskilled miners won strike after strike in the later 1890s, the wily "craft" unionists applauded their success and welcomed into the AFL the United Mine Workers of America. This was a national union which ignored the distinction between craftsmen and laborers. Pragmatism as well as the development of a "job conscious" philosophy accounted for the rise of the AFL.

The Leadership of Samuel Gompers

In developing a more flexible philosophy of job conscious unionism, the AFL owed much to the leadership of its first president, Samuel Gompers. With the exception of one year, 1895, Gompers was annually elected AFL president from 1886 until his death in 1924. He was born in London of Dutch-Jewish parents and at an early age was apprenticed to a cigarmaker. Although exposed to Socialist influences after his family moved to New York in 1863, Gompers always preferred loyalty to his immediate circle to any idea of class solidarity. He remembered the advice given to him by one European revolutionary: "Study your union card, Sam, and if the idea doesn't square with that, it ain't true."

In 1864 Gompers joined the Cigarmakers' Union, an organization which he subsequently helped to rebuild after the depression of the 1870s into one of the most powerful of national unions. When he was president of Local No. 144 in New York City, he became involved in a bitter dispute with the Knights of Labor over which labor union should have jurisdiction in his trade. Thereafter, as president of the AFL, Gompers devoted his considerable diplomatic skills to an attempt to avert "dual unionism" and jurisdictional disputes which might damage the cause of organized labor. He also made his influence felt in opposing any alliance between the labor movement and

Contributing largely to the success of the American Federation of Labor was the fact that its president and founder was a man of high principles. And Samuel Gompers (above) would not mix labor with politics.

intellectuals, Socialists, or politicians of any hue. In his opinion, laboring men were best advised to rely upon their own economic experience and strength. The executive powers of the AFL president were, however, limited. Each craft within the AFL was autonomous; affiliated unions were not obliged to take Gompers's advice, and the president himself was forced to accept various unions' policies, like political action, of which he disapproved.

Gompers and the AFL did not entirely disapprove of political action. Craft unionists recognized a need to lobby in Congress and in state legislatures for laws which would protect their organizations. When the AFL was formed, there was widespread concern over the need for an eight-hour day on federal work projects, laws to prevent "shanghaiing" or the forcible recruitment of Americans as sailors. There was also concern for legislation needed to prevent the granting of court injunctions which, upon an unsupported allegation of union coercion, could be used to tie up labor's funds during a strike. To pursue such goals the AFL set up a permanent lobbying committee in 1895. Various state federations of labor, formed in the 1890s, paralleled the work of their parent body by lobbying state legislatures, thus performing some of the functions of labor parties in other countries.

Although the connection between labor and politics was comparatively weak by the 1890s, it was founded upon significant precedents. In the post-Civil War years, the "butternuts," or soft money interests, had risen in rebellion against political domination by the hard money "bondocracy." Their complaint was that big business was conspiring to deflate the economy by urging the government to reduce the number of "greenback" dollars in circulation, a policy which made life difficult for farmers, who thrived on easy credit and inflation. In response to the depression of the 1870s, and to the hostile attitude of the government during the popular railroad strikes of 1877, members of the Knights and of national labor unions joined the farmers to form the Greenback-Labor party. The Greenbackers demanded not only currency reform, but also concessions to labor, such as legislation ensuring the eight-hour day. Their candidates received a million votes in 1878, Powderly being elected mayor of Scranton, Pennsylvania, in the face of a smear campaign which described him as the candidate of the "Molly Maguire Ticket."

The overwhelming defeat of James B. Weaver, Greenback-Labor candidate for the 1880 presidential election, showed that the farmer-labor combination had serious weaknesses. The reasons for the dissolution of the alliance are clear. Currency reform had by 1880 diminished the discontent of the farmers. Industrial revival made the urban workers complacent. The Democratic party made a successful play for the labor vote. These factors were enough to destroy the farmer-labor alliance because it was in any case strained. Inflationary policies might have helped the farmers, but they would have injured workers whose wages were much more rigid than the prices of farm products. Farmers and urban workers also tended to quarrel because, as Gompers later pointed out, farmers were property-owning employers who favored collective action only in dire emergencies.

Another political precedent for the AFL leaders was the Workingmen's party of California. The party was organized in opposition to Chinese immigration, which had begun in the 1850s and by the 1870s accounted for a quarter of California wage earners. "Coolie" labor was cheap. When it threatened to displace white labor during the hard times of the 1870s, the demagogic Denis Kearney of San Francisco first tried to force the Chinese out of jobs with the aid of his "pick-handle brigade" of roving thugs, and then resorted to politics. The federal law of 1882 excluding Chinese immigration met the demands of his Workingmen's party. The law reflected the way in which California labor, cut off from the rest of the United States, could unite on a state-wide political basis and exert effective pressure on Washington.

Although heavily concentrated in California, anti-Chinese sentiment spread to other states. This riot in Denver in the 1880s shows the terrorist tactics used by whites to bully Chinese in that city.

The aim of the Workingmen's party was to make labor more valuable by restricting the supply from abroad. Such an aim was consistent with the scarcity-oriented ideology of the AFL. Gompers went further and endorsed the racial overtones of Chinese exclusion, maintaining in 1901 that "every incoming coolie means . . . so much more vice and immorality injected into our social life." The racial issue on the West Coast had been kept alive in the meantime by anti-Chinese riots and by the further problem of Japanese immigration. But, while the AFL endorsed the racial demands of the white workers of California, it did not apply on a nationwide basis the technique of third-party organization. Gompers and his fellow officials in the American Federation of Labor were fully aware of the fact that political cooperation would have been far more difficult to achieve on the national level, where one could not rely, as one could in the West Coast, on the unifying effects of that "indispensable enemy," coolie labor.

Protection for the Workers

In addition to Gompers's attitude, there were other reasons for the poor political showing of the American Left prior to 1900. The enmity of the Catholic Church and the opportunities for advancement which existed in America undermined class consciousness. Job consciousness flourished in a country which, until 1900, offered a high and comparatively stable standard of living. There were, however, exceptions to the general prosperity. In a political democracy, those who could not retaliate at the polls were at a disadvantage. Migrants, recent immigrants, blacks, women, and children formed poorly paid minorities in the wage-earning force. They were relatively unskilled. In industries where machinery and invention were eliminating the need for apprenticeship, women and children easily found employment. In Gompers's trade, cigarmaking, half the workers were women and children in 1900, and the proportion was rising. Women and children employed in manufacturing received only about half the remuneration which male workers received.

In 1891 Pope Leo XIII issued an encyclical urging protection for the workers. This Joseph Keppler cartoon mockingly portrays the Catholic Church lending support to the Knights of Labor.

Those who were male, white, adult, and settled enjoyed an advantage. But they were never entirely free from anxiety. While some labor unions ran health benefit schemes, sickness usually meant financial disaster in a family. Safety regulations in industry came only with patience and experience; an industrial accident to the head of a household in the nineteenth century meant penury. If a worker avoided the all-too-frequent industrial accident, he could still expect with some certainty spells of unemployment which in each year might last for days, weeks, or months. It was a tiny if noble handful of employers and unions which ran private unemployment insurance schemes. Gompers's solution to the problem of unemployment was a shorter working day with more men put to work. The ten-hour day had, in fact, been achieved in most industries by 1890. There was, however, a humanitarian reason as well as an economic one for pressing on with the demand for shorter hours in the 1890s. In the absence of uniform legislation, some occupations did not conform to national standards. Men still worked up to eighty-four hours a week in the physi-

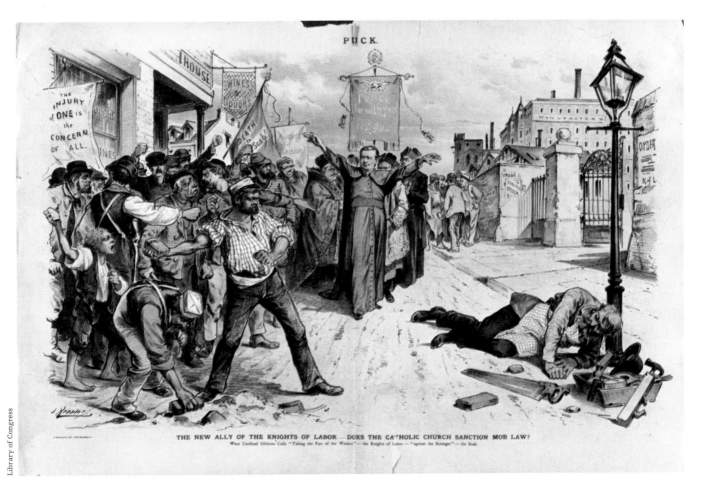

THE NEW ALLY OF THE KNIGHTS OF LABOR—DOES THE CATHOLIC CHURCH SANCTION MOB LAW?

George Eastman House

Child labor was a major target for reformers and trade unionists. Lewis Hine submitted this evocative photograph to a committee on labor reform, as a silent witness in his campaign to end the practice.

cally trying steel industry. They aged prematurely. Yet, until the Arizona law of 1915 which pioneered old-age insurance, there was no state provision for retirement pensions.

The nineteenth-century attack on social insecurity included little federal action. One of the exceptions was a law which Congress passed in 1868 restricting the working day to eight hours on federal projects, but even this legislation was ineffective until it was strengthened in 1892. The social reform initiative came chiefly from individual states, particularly from those which were industrially mature. Massachusetts, for example, passed a law regulating child labor as early as 1836, and in 1866 the Bay State established the first factory inspection system.

Social reform legislation, which aimed at the common good, was distinguishable from labor legislation, which often aimed to improve the condition only of that "aristo-cracy of labor" which was organized into unions. Labor unions did support public measures which would benefit their members, particularly reforms in education,

suffrage, the homesteading system, and immigration restriction. Their lobby for legislation protecting women and children was, however, guided by self-interest as well as by principle. This emotive demand won widespread support; and by 1900, twenty-eight states prohibited by law the employment of children under twelve, while thir-teen restricted the hours of female toil to eight a day. Such reforms commanded the support of labor unions because they diminished the extent of wage-undercutting. Moreover, it was a nineteenth-century jibe that the male textile workers of Massachusetts were exploiting chivalry. They intended to "fight the battle from behind the women's petticoats" and to secure for themselves conditions first conceded to their wives and daughters.

A good deal of the labor legislation sought by unions was specifically designed to help their own members. The AFL's legislative objective in the 1890s was, indeed, little more than the protection of the right to organize. Whereas the Knights of Labor had pressed for broad political objectives in the 1880s, the AFL and its affiliates sought narrower concessions like immunity from court injunc-tions and from conspiracy proceedings. The flood of social reform legislation which had gained strength since the Civil War now lost its impetus. Nevertheless, there were hundreds of laws already on the statute books by 1890,

Passed by Grant in 1868, the first eight-hour law applied only to federal employees. This poster was hung in the Mare Island, California, naval yard to boost the morale of its workers.

and in the twentieth century the reform flood spilled over onto the national level. The labor movement at the end of the century had paved the way for change.

It may be argued that the caution of the AFL in the 1890s reflected the economic and political realities of the time. The United States was so prosperous that the working class formed a permanent minority of the population, a circumstance which limited the effectiveness of labor politics. Indeed, few wage earners thought of themselves as working class in status and only a small minority belonged to labor unions. Employers were economically strong, and in 1895 they combined in the National Association of Manufacturers to defend their interests. The coal and railroad magnate George F. Baer expressed in 1902 the employers' hostility to unions in an outburst which became retrospectively notorious: "The rights and interests of the laboring man will be protected and cared for—not by the labor agitators, but by the Christian men to whom God in his infinite wisdom has given control of the property interests of this country."

The power of organized labor was further limited by the hostility of government. AFL leaders were aggrieved by the regularity with which presidents and governors mobilized troops to "break" strikes. Just as frustrating was the adverse legal environment with which unions had to contend. The most egalitarian measures were susceptible to "interpretation" in the courts. The Fourteenth Amendment to the Constitution, designed to help black Americans, was used instead to uphold the freedom of contract principle, whereby state laws regulating conditions of employment were held invalid. The Sherman Antitrust Act of 1890, aimed at business monoplies, was applied in practice to the harassment of labor unions. Discouraging court decisions reflected the intent of the framers of the Constitution—and the inevitable bias of judges who had served their apprenticeships as corporation lawyers.

The limited extent of union power at the end of the nineteenth century reflected in part the economic and political obstacles which workingmen faced. On the other hand, it is impossible to win a battle without committing one's troops to the fray. The AFL never fully committed itself to a political program, to the organization of blacks, or to the recruitment of the unskilled. Such restraint was not entirely imposed by outside factors. Some governors, like Altgeld of Illinois, and some presidents, like Theodore Roosevelt, tolerated and indeed encouraged the rise of labor. In 1898, the Supreme Court upheld the Utah eight-hour-day law. It was just as these warmer zephyrs of the twentieth century wafted over the labor movement that Gompers lashed its helm as if to weather the chill gales of the 1880s.

Chapter 4

A CULTURE IN TRANSITION

America's greatly increased wealth in the industrial age meant that the ideal of publicly financed education for all could be extended to high school and college level. Private donors, too, built libraries, art galleries, and concert halls in obedience to Andrew Carnegie's "gospel of wealth." Together with the huge fairs in Philadelphia and Chicago, these enterprises created great opportunities for the nation's new architects. But the confident and assertive mood of the buildings they designed was not echoed by artists in other fields. Public taste often did not appreciate either the realistic or the impressionistic painting of the age, while writers were torn between confidence and the bleak reality they often saw around them in American society.

A Creative Age

Each generation is apt to dislike the immediately preceding one. With the passage of time it too falls into disfavor, and its standards of taste—or distaste—are then overturned. So with the period from 1865 to 1900, dubbed the "Gilded Age" by Mark Twain. For several decades in the twentieth century, this American era was often dismissed as a cultural and intellectual wasteland. According to the historian Samuel Eliot Morison, it was a period when "the clank of machinery and the clink of dollars silenced religion, letters, and the arts." The architectural writer Lewis Mumford christened these years *The Brown Decades*. In such depictions the genius of a small band of writers, artists, and thinkers appeared as a usually hopeless struggle against vulgarity, conformism, and sheer indifference. The atmosphere, we are told, was poisonous for the creative spirit; the choice was either to supply the public appetite for sentimental or pompous stuff, or else to be misunderstood and neglected. In this view, the great American middle class was greedy and indiscriminate. Americans led cluttered, hypocritical lives. "Provided there is space to move about without knocking over the furniture," a book on interior decoration advised them, "there is hardly likely to be too much in the room." What hope for brilliance and candor in those genteel, gaslit parlors? Among the casualties of the Gilded Age, it used to be said, were the poet Emily Dickinson, practically unknown when she died in Amherst, Massachusetts, in 1886; Herman Melville, whose funeral in 1891 was barely noticed in the newspapers; and the painter Albert Pinkham Ryder, working away in isolation in New York.

There is a partial truth in this interpretation. Indeed the problem was admitted by contemporaries. The novelist William Dean Howells said ruefully that Americans after the Civil War had, "as no other people in the world had, the chance of devoting ourselves strictly to business, of buying cheap and selling dear." Complacency and commercialism are always rife, and in the Gilded Age success in business was vastly admired. A prodigious amount of energy went into material pursuits. In comparison with twentieth-century America, the national achievement in more purely intellectual or artistic fields was perhaps not world-shaking. Not much, for example, was yet coming out of the United States by way of music or drama. Most of the great theoretical work in science was still being done in Europe. Americans continued to look across the Atlantic for training or inspiration. Young scholars assured one another that Germany was the best place for universities. Painters, sculptors, and architects made pilgrimages to Paris or Rome. Some Americans, including the novelist Henry James and the painter Mary Cassatt, settled in Europe because they felt the conditions for creative work were more pleasant than at home.

But it would be quite wrong to conclude that intellect and imagination were lacking in the United States. Certain issues seemed to matter less than in Europe. On the whole Americans believed they had solved the essential problems of democratic government, over which Europeans were still arguing. With rather less unanimity they tended to believe they had also hit upon the most effective economic system: *laissez-faire*, meaning private enterprise with a minimum of government control. Socialist ideas were therefore left mainly to Europeans to formulate. Otherwise the great questions of the time occupied the thinking of Europeans and Americans alike. The world was growing more complicated: was complexity a proof of progress, or a sign of impending chaos? Science was acquiring more and more prestige: did its findings support or undermine religious faith? Individualism seemed basic to human freedom: how could it be reconciled with the needs of the whole community? Did mankind actually possess free will, or were human actions predetermined by biological, economic, and other factors? New discoveries and theories suggested new conceptions of reality. How should the artist or writer define "reality"? Was it his duty to present the unvarnished truth, or to provide uplift, or to offer people a romantic escape from everyday existence? These and some related themes were subject to intense debate in various spheres. The answers that Americans proposed were often ingenious or sensible, though in their nature none could be final. Certainly they did not sustain the picture of an entire nation of soulless money-grubbers.

The Benefits of Wealth

The previous, hostile characterization of the Gilded Age can actually be restated in much more favorable terms. The argument would then run that American culture thrived not *in spite of* but *because of* economic circumstance. In world history, scholarship and creative excellence have flourished in societies whose wealth, power, and confidence were on the increase. By 1900 the United States was the richest nation in the world, measured in total assets and in per capita income; and the graphs of production were obviously going to continue soaring. For the majority of the population, though of course not for everybody, this swift and unmistakable surge was exhilarating. It induced a mood of optimism, of boldness, of possibility—an insistence on the best that money could buy, whatever that might be. Historically, culture has depended upon patronage: the readiness of wealth to support the arts and learning. In the United States the wealth was becoming available. The client need no longer fall back upon the skills of Europe, for native expertise was now undeniable. The millionaire was anxious to lay out his (largely untaxed) income in ways that would gratify him.

Also, the rich in America were frequently anxious to display their pride in their own cities, and to put their money to public use. As early as the 1830s, Americans had shown that they did not mind others acquiring money, provided that the fortunate few gave back a substantial proportion in philanthropy. Stephen Girard, a rich Philadelphian who died in 1831, was praised by everybody when his will revealed that he had left several million dollars to improve his city and endow a college. John Jacob Astor, who died in 1848, was assailed for not leaving any big bequest for public benefits. A New York newspaper claimed that at least half his fortune had "accrued to him by the industry of the community," and so ought to have been given to the city.

America's post-Civil War rich had learned this lesson. The doctrine as expounded by the steel multimillionaire Andrew Carnegie in his "gospel of wealth" was that each man of means should hold his estate as a steward or trustee, disposing of it for the general good. Libraries and education came at the top of Carnegie's personal list. These were keys to knowledge, and so to power and wealth. Others agreed with him. Their endowments, and their impulse to back educational institutions, coincided with a great national upsurge of renewed enthusiasm. At state level, there was almost universal agreement that common schooling should be properly financed. The establishment of high schools was a more expensive proposition. Inevitably the more prosperous states pushed ahead faster than the poorer, more thinly populated ones in the West and South. New York, Ohio, or Illinois were well in advance of, say, Mississippi or the Dakotas. Even so the public high school, in state after state, became a standard feature rather than a luxury. As provision for primary and secondary schooling spread, the private academies which had before 1865 been the dominant institutions began to fall away. In the 1880s, for the first time in America's history, more children were receiving public than private education; and the trend continued.

The vigor of public education was equally apparent beyond the high-school stage. State universities such as Michigan which had had to struggle in their early days now moved boldly forward. They chose redoubtable men —James B. Angell at Michigan, Charles Kendall Adams at Wisconsin—as presidents. California launched its state university in 1869, luring Daniel Coit Gilman from the East to be one of its distinguished run of overlords. Several of these foundations insisted that their role was

Public elementary schools had been established
almost everywhere by the late nineteenth century,
but the amount of money available varied from state
to state. Right: Edward Henry Lamson's Country School.

Yale University Art Gallery. The Mabel Brady Garvan Collection

College Days

Nineteenth-century fortunes were frequently donated for educational purposes. Ezra Cornell, chief stockholder in Western Union and state senator for New York, gave his millions toward the founding of the university that bears his name. The institution was founded in 1865. Right: The trappings of campus life are on display in this turn-of-the-century dormitory room. Left: Varsity crew on Ithaca's Lake Cayuga. Above left: In 1873 dress, the freshman crew. Above center: Football team, 1895. Above right: Dr James Law conducts his horse anatomy class, 1894.

to serve the public good in every conceivable fashion. Adams of Wisconsin, foreshadowing what became known as the "Wisconsin Idea," proclaimed in 1896: "The university is not a party separate from the State. It is a part of the State—as much a part . . . as the Capitol itself —as much as the brain and the hand are parts of the body." This was, too, the avowed aim of the state land-grant "A & M" (Agricultural & Mechanical) colleges brought into being by the Morrill Act of 1862. They were intended to provide free or at any rate very cheap training for budding farmers and engineers. The vocational emphasis was understandably strong. But this did not mean there was no place for culture in state universities and colleges. Willa Cather, later a famous novelist, was able to take courses in Latin and Greek when she was a freshman at the University of Nebraska in 1890. Even in small towns like Red Cloud, where she attended high school, there were cultivated people to talk to; and the Red Cloud Opera House drew good audiences for visiting theatrical troupes.

Privately financed education was equally vigorous. The eagerness, to repeat, was already there; money simply strengthened and accelerated development. Soon after the Civil War, several well-known existing colleges began to reform and expand. Their intention was epitomized by Charles W. Eliot, a chemist appointed to the presidency of Harvard in 1869: "No object of human inquiry can be out of place in the programme of a real university." A real university must be big, cover the whole range of scholarship, and introduce graduate schools. Harvard, Yale, and (more slowly) Columbia and Princeton were transformed into large, ambitious, bustling enterprises. In part they were stimulated by the challenge of brand-new universities. Cornell, whose first president was the Michigan history professor Andrew D. White, opened in 1868—half a Morrill land-grant product and half the result of a substantial gift from the telegraph millionaire Ezra Cornell. "I would found an institution," said Cornell, "where any person can find instruction in any study." Within a few years there was a formidable new rival, again the product of private philanthropy, in the shape of Johns Hopkins University in Baltimore. Hopkins, whose early postgraduates included the historian Frederick Jackson Turner and the political scientist Woodrow Wilson, joined in stressing the seminar method and the PhD—both of these to some extent German imports. The new type of professor was a professional specialist, no longer expected to conduct classes in half a dozen different subjects. History, language study, sociology, anthropology, psychology, philosophy, economics, physics, chemistry emerged as separate disciplines, each with its subdivisions, its national association, and its scholarly magazines. In each branch American academics began to acquire world reputations, combining Germanic thoroughness with a native freshness of approach. Yale, for

example, had Willard Gibbs, now commonly regarded as America's greatest physicist of the nineteenth century. Harvard's philosophy department brought together the dazzling talents of William James (brother of the novelist Henry James), Josiah Royce, and George Santayana. Frederick Jackson Turner became one of the stars of the Wisconsin faculty. Woodrow Wilson—who also helped to coach football—made a name at Wesleyan and Princeton. Private endowments brought three more universities into being between 1889 and 1892: Chicago, the protégé of John D. Rockefeller; Clark, in Worcester, Massachusetts; and Leland Stanford, Jr in California, from which Herbert Hoover graduated as a mining engineer.

State institutions were coeducational from the start. So were a sprinkling of private colleges such as Oberlin. Fully fledged colleges for women were mainly a creation of the post-1865 period, usually the outcome of philanthropy. This was the case with Vassar (1865), Wellesley (1870), Smith (1875), and Bryn Mawr (1885). By 1900 about 100,000 women were in college, or attending state normal schools as teacher-trainees. Considerably more men were receiving higher education. But the opportunities for American women were better than anywhere else in the world.

Private wealth and local patriotism, singly or in combination, had other impressive effects. Many millions of dollars were spent on public libraries, with Carnegie only one of the donors. In the late 1890s the process was climaxed by the formation of the New York Public Library, and the opening of the splendid new Library of Congress, together with magnificent library buildings in Boston and Chicago. Symphony orchestras were formed, with solid backing (New York, 1878; Boston, 1881; Chicago, 1891). Grand opera obtained a glittering American headquarters with the completion of New York's Metropolitan Opera House in 1883. This was the era also when city after city established art academies and museums—and when rich individuals were beginning to assemble private art collections which would eventually be willed to public galleries. Work began on Boston's Old Art Museum in 1872. The same decade saw the construction of the Metropolitan Museum in New York, of which the first portion was opened in 1880.

The quality of life in American cities grew worse and better, both at once. There was a spread of crowded, squalid slums. On the other hand there were handsome new churches, banks, clubs, department stores, hotels, office blocks, lawcourts, concert halls, and open spaces such as New York's Central Park. There were elegant mansions for the rich—in fashionable central districts, in spacious suburbs, and in flourishing summer-resort communities like Newport, Rhode Island.

The situation brought extraordinary chances for American architects, and for sculptors. Critics of the nineteenth century's latter decades once ridiculed the

Turning his back to the painting, the young boy in this party is clearly not impressed by Washington Crossing the Delaware. *But the opening of the Metropolitan Museum of Art in New York City in 1880 allowed millions of ordinary people to share more fully in the nation's cultural heritage.*

era for borrowing styles, and sometimes mixing them up in weird blends, instead of hitting upon a style of its own. It is in truth hard not to be startled by some of the overblown art and architecture displayed, say, at the Philadelphia Centennial Exposition of 1876, or the Chicago World's Fair of 1893. The colossal statues, the fountains full of writhing bronze nymphs, the riot of ornament look hideous to people whose preference is for simplicity in design. In defense of the United States of the Gilded Age, we can say that popular taste is never "refined" in any age; that Europe revealed exactly the same appetites; and that, viewed by its own standards, a great deal of what was produced has important merits.

The New Architecture

One of the main debates among architects was whether to build in "Gothic" or in "Romanesque." The Gothic style favored pointed windows and a spired roof line, and a generally intricate, church like appearance. The American version of Romanesque opted for rounded windows and doorways, and a lower and simpler overall shape. The latter principle triumphed in the work of America's first architect of genius, Henry Hobson Richardson. Richardson's Trinity Church, Boston, begun in 1872, won him all the commissions he could handle in his brief, meteoric career (he died in 1886 when he was only forty-seven). His big essays—city halls, railroad

stations, university auditoriums—were massive, almost squat granite piles, yet strangely graceful. The Chicago architect Louis Sullivan, a genius of another order, paid tribute to Richardson's seven-story Marshall Field building (finished in 1885, demolished in 1930). "Four-square and brown it stands, a monument to . . . the organized commercial spirit, to the power and progress of the age, to the strength and resource of individuality of character."

Richardson dominated American architecture in the 1870s and 1880s. The best among his followers and imitators was the firm of McKim, Mead, and White, who set up their New York office in 1879. Charles Follen McKim and Stanford White had worked for Richardson. Like Richardson, the flamboyant White was a man of varied artistic gifts. He designed magazine covers for *Scribner's, Century,* and other publications. He was a close friend of the sculptor Augustus Saint-Gaudens, creator of the beautiful "Striding Liberty" $20 gold piece.

A French visitor to the Chicago World's Fair was not impressed by the wedding-cake ornateness of the "White City." The main committee of architects had decided to follow "the pure ideal of the ancients," even though this meant applying the whiteness with a squirt-gun. But one "fantastic construction" caught the French critic's eye. It was red in color, and "of a studied roughness. . . . One could see in it . . . a dream of new forms which would harmonize with the tumultuous and brutal genius of . . . Chicago." This was Louis Sullivan's Transportation Building, the fair's solitary architectural masterpiece. Sullivan himself did not suffer fools gladly. He denounced the fair

More than 27 million people toured the exhibits of Chicago's Columbian Exposition (1893). The White City (inset) struck some as too ornate, although most of the visitors applauded its formality. More significant, but not as popular, was Louis Sullivan's Transportation Building (below).

*In addition to enhancing the Chicago world's fair
in 1893, Louis Sullivan pioneered the skyscraper.
One of the earliest was Buffalo's Guaranty Building
(1894), designed by Sullivan and Dankmar Adler.*

all stimulated the concept of the "skyscraper," which was pioneered in Chicago. The tall office building, Sullivan declared, "must be every inch a proud and soaring thing, . . . a unit without a single dissenting line." With his partner Dankmar Adler, Sullivan achieved skyscraper miracles such as the Wainwright Building in St Louis (1891) and Buffalo's Guaranty Building (1895). In Chicago their triumphs included the sumptuous Auditorium, whose opening concert was attended in 1889 by the president of the United States. The Adler-Sullivan partnership did not hold together, and Sullivan died a disappointed man. The organic modernists in architecture had, he felt, lost the battle to the reproducers of stale Greek and Roman motifs. In a way he was correct. Even in a new city, or perhaps because it was such a "shock city," most people wanted to be comforted rather than puzzled by the buildings around them. But his own insights were prophetic. A youngster named Frank Lloyd Wright, who came to work in Sullivan's office in 1887 and opened his own firm in 1893, was to carry the Sullivan revolution forward with still greater courage and genius.

The Realm of Ideas

Sullivan's French admirer called Chicago "tumultuous and brutal." Similar words were often used to describe the whole nature of modern existence, especially in the United States. And often the discussion revolved around the idea of evolution as expounded in England by Charles Darwin and Herbert Spencer. Darwin's *Origin of Species* (1859) was too technically complicated to be readily absorbed by the average man, though Asa Gray of Harvard and some other American scientists immediately grasped the Darwinian theory. But the gist of the theory, and the possibly ominous implications, were clear enough. Darwinism offered an answer for one of the riddles of the universe: why were there so many different species of plant and animal life, some of them linked in various families? The old explanation was that they had been simultaneously created by God, more or less as indicated in the book of Genesis. But evidence had been piling up to suggest that some species had become extinct, while others had "evolved" or changed their characteristics. Darwin's view was that evolution had come about through "natural selection": in other words, the accidental adaptation to environment—or, in Spencer's phrase, the "survival of the fittest." Defenseless creatures like butterflies had developed protective devices such as camouflage. Predatory creatures had become more effective by developing greater agility and muscle, and sharper teeth. This immense process had continued through countless generations, according to its own blind logic.

Where then did God, and mankind, fit into the scheme

as an architectural disaster, an opportunity thrown away. The American public, thronging to the White City in millions, did not agree with him. They were enchanted by the gleaming elaborate pavilions. But Sullivan and the French observer spoke with the voice of the future. An American style, or more particularly a Chicago style, was trying to be born. It would be native, and modern, and democratic—a first-hand statement and not an echo from the past. Sullivan wanted his buildings to match the poems of Walt Whitman in their unforced, natural originality. Chicago seemed the right place. It was a new city, growing by leaps and bounds, much of the center gutted by the great fire of 1871. Steel-frame construction, the invention of the elevator, and the daunting cost of land of things? If man had evolved from the ape, how could he be in any sense an angel? There seemed to be no room for the divine spark, no purpose in life—only unending biological strife. For many, evolution at first was a grimly unacceptable doctrine. The challenge was particularly disturbing for clergymen and others with strong religious convictions. Gradually, though, Darwinism spread. America's celebrated preachers, including Henry Ward Beecher, began to comfort their congregations with the thought that evolution was after all compatible with the word of God. Darwin himself was a sincere Christian. James McCosh, lecturing at Union Theological Seminary in 1870, claimed that scriptural and evolutionary accounts of creation were in broad agreement. "In both, the inanimate comes before the animal; in both, the grass and

Ragged Dick was just one of Horatio Alger's heroes whose life was a progression from "rags to riches." But it could work the other way: Alger himself squandered the fortune he made in writing and died poor.

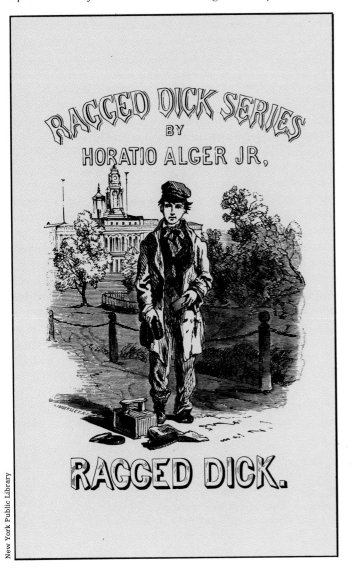

herb and trees, before the animal. . . . In both, we have as the last of the train, man standing upright and facing the sky." Not everyone was so easily convinced. The Reverend DeWitt Talmage of Brooklyn, almost as popular a spellbinder as Beecher, poured scorn on evolutionism. Talmage's reaction to a public dinner given for Spencer in New York in 1882 was: "There the banqueters sat around the table in honor of Herbert Spencer, chewing beef, turkey, and roast pig, which, according to their doctrine of evolution, made them eating their own relations!" More reasoned opposition came from Gray's Harvard colleague, the immensely learned scientist Louis Agassiz.

But Agassiz died in 1873, and by 1900 outright opposition to Darwinism was confined to religious fundamentalists who insisted that the Bible was literally, not just metaphorically, true. Evolution was fairly and fully debated and was held as dogma by figures as far removed as Andrew Carnegie and the Yale sociologist William Graham Sumner. Darwinian ideas, when encountered by the young novelists Theodore Dreiser and Jack London, struck them with the force of a revelation. In the guise of "Social Darwinism," evolution was thus applied to human society. As such it did not so much overturn as reinforce the attitudes of a nation that already set store by hard work, competition, and self-help. Social Darwinism confirmed the impression that the rich were rich, and the poor poor, because they deserved to be. The survival of the fittest was a law of nature. The poor could be helped by indirect philanthropy, of the Carnegie type—but not by direct charity, which would only sap their will. Carnegie's own rise from poverty to boundless wealth was cited as proof that a deserving lad could go and do the same. This was the theme of the scores of paperback novelettes churned out in the "Ragged Dick," "Luck and Pluck," and "Tattered Tom" series by the ex-clergyman Horatio Alger between 1867 and the late 1890s.

At a more sophisticated level, Social Darwinism was dinned into Yale students by the tough-minded Sumner. "This is a world," he told them, "in which the rule is 'Root, hog, or die'." Any interference with social evolution would do harm. "Let it be understood that we cannot get outside this alternative: liberty, inequality, survival of the fittest; non-liberty, equality, survival of the unfittest. The former carries society forward and favors all its best members; the latter carries society downwards and favors all its worst members." America's "Forgotten Man," he wrote in an essay of that title, was the ordinary American who toiled to support himself and his family, asked no favors, and was taxed for the benefit of the lazy and incompetent. Yet the process was not only inevitable, it was desirable. Evolution guaranteed improvement—at least for the Carnegies: Sumner was less optimistic.

Sumner refused to be horrified by the vision of the city

as an asphalt jungle. Men, he thought, had always been subject to the same savage necessity. But some American thinkers drew opposite conclusions from the doctrine of evolution. They have been called "Reform Darwinists." What they had in common was the belief that human beings were infinitely more complicated than animals. Human society was artificial. Being man-made, it could be man-*altered* by the application of intelligence and collective decency. The anthropologist Lewis Henry Morgan ended his book *Ancient Society* (1877) with the prediction that "democracy in government, brotherhood in society, equality in rights and privileges, and universal education, foreshadow the next higher plane of society to which experience, intelligence, and knowledge are tending." The sociologist Lester Frank Ward, who like Sumner had been born poor, contended in *Dynamic Sociology* (1883) that society and nature could not properly be compared. The element of intellect, morality, forethought, and cooperation in human beings had replaced the law of nature with the "law of mind." Was not civilization, he asked, "the result of man's *not* letting things alone, and of his *not* letting nature take its course?" Farm crops and animals, the product of man's conscious interference, were much "fitter" or better than in their "natural" origins. The logic of human or social evolution led toward final victory over "the competitive egoism that all men have inherited from their animal ancestors." *Laissez-faire* was bad history and bad ethics. Men had a responsibility to aid one another. This kind of interpre-

tation proved increasingly congenial, as the century wore away, to Americans of good will who had become alarmed by the callous impersonality of modern industrial metropolises like Chicago.

Art and Literature

As among scholars, so among artists and writers there was a tension between optimism and pessimism, charm and candor, acceptance and protest: a tension not yet resolved when the century closed.

In painting and sculpture the general public taste remained somewhat conventional and romantic. The most popular art, as displayed at the Philadelphia and Chicago expositions, was carefully rendered landscape and portraiture, together with historical scenes and whimsical or melodramatic pictures that "told a story." Art should be artistic: that was agreed. It should also be "lifelike." But what was "life"? Thomas Moran's huge *Chasm of the Colorado* was attacked by an *Atlantic Monthly* critic in 1874 who declared: "The only aim of art is to feed the sense of beauty; it has no right to meddle with horrors and desolations." The less bleak landscapes of George Inness were more appealing. So were the dazzlingly accomplished portraits of John Singer Sargent, though later they began to verge on slickness. James McNeill Whistler, who spent most of his time in Paris and London, offended the critics with his brand of impressionism— and even more perhaps with his sharp tongue. Winslow Homer, who stayed in America, was also not renowned for amiability. He responded to demands for his autograph by pulling out a rubber-stamp facsimile. But he contrived to paint oils and watercolors, especially of seascapes, that were memorably truthful to the quality of light between sky and water.

At the beginning of the era, nudes were not considered respectable, unless perhaps as statuary. Paintings of nude women were not salon but saloon art—hanging over the bar for male customers to eye. The convention persisted that clad figures were more "lifelike" than naked ones. Thomas Eakins of Philadelphia, arguably the greatest American artist of the era, ran into trouble when he insisted on drawing from the nude. "Respectability in art," he once remarked, "is appalling." Not that his aim was to be sensational: he simply wanted to be honest.

Courtesy of the Jefferson Medical College, Thomas Jefferson University (detail)

The Philadelphian Thomas Eakins studied both fine art and anatomy. Left: The Gross Clinic *raised eyebrows when it appeared (1865). James Whistler uprooted himself from the United States at twenty-one to live in Europe, mostly in Paris and London. His devoted mistress, Joanna Heffernan, posed for* The Little White Girl: Symphony in White No. 2 *(right).*

"That's the way it looked to me" was another of his comments. He was fascinated in an almost scientific way by anatomy—the theme of his finely serious study of a surgical operation, *The Clinic of Dr Gross* (1875). He was fascinated by the motion photographs of Eadweard Muybridge, which for the very first time revealed the actual sequence of movements of the human body. Eakins caught the poetry as well as the technique of athletic activity in some paintings of men rowing on the Schuylkill River. Eakins's deep honesty, and his pleasure in outdoor pastimes, have ensured permanence for his art where some of his more stylish contemporaries have ceased to speak to us. Some of Winslow Homer's New England and

Caribbean scenes have likewise kept their authority for us.

American writing achieved more than the run of visual art. The three major authors were William Dean Howells, Mark Twain, and Henry James. Howells stood in the middle. He was a friend of Twain and of James—whereas Twain and James were unacquainted and probably would not have warmed to one another. All three however, in the postwar years, wanted to be "realists." For the more bookish Howells and James this meant defining and sticking to a quite precise code of rules. They believed that novels should be well constructed and firmly shaped —on French and Russian models rather than like what

James called the "loose, baggy monsters" of English fiction such as those of Charles Dickens. In real life, they recognized, there are no totally villainous people. Events were apt to be untidy; amazing coincidences and set-piece encounters were rare. Wedding bells did not signify that a couple would live happily ever after. In their plots they tried to be faithful to their principles. James's *Portrait of a Lady* (1881) and Howells's *A Modern Instance* (1882) both deal with unhappy marriages. Howells's best novel, *The Rise of Silas Lapham* (1885), deals with a heroine who is not pretty and a parent who is clumsy and not very likable. Twain's first novels, up to his supreme work *The Adventures of Huckleberry Finn*

(1884), were less deliberate in technique. Mark Twain, with his superb ear for language and his comedian's gift of exaggeration, achieved realism through a mixture of mimicry and satire. His talent was too personal, and too uneven, to fit any neat formula. Nor indeed can we make much sense of Henry James by dubbing him a realist. What he and Twain did share, in a broad sense, was deep involvement in the techniques of writing, and a scorn for

In his early career as an artist, Winslow Homer recorded Civil War scenes for Harper's Weekly. *Later he turned his attention to the sea. His vivid oil* Breezing Up *dates from 1875.*

Henry James (left, in a portrait by John Singer Sargent) was an active writer for well over fifty years. Among his most important novels were The Portrait of a Lady *and* The Ambassadors. *Stephen Crane (above) died aged twenty-nine. He won instant fame with* The Red Badge of Courage.

fraudulence. Twain was like a firework display—dazzling and delightful, but now and then apt to misfire or get out of control.

In the middle was their mutual friend Howells, an editor first of the *Atlantic Monthly* in Boston and then of *Harper's* in New York. He is a key figure for anyone who wants to understand the mind of the Gilded Age. His early conception of realism was expressed in the much-quoted statement that "our novelists . . . concern themselves with the more smiling aspects of life, which are the more American. . . . It is worth while, even at the risk of being called commonplace, to be true to our well-to-do actualities." Howells was not saying that everyone in the United States was rich and carefree. His notion was that America, rather, was a place without violent extremes. He saw that it was hard for a novelist to catch the essence of life when no one was an aristocrat or a serf, but something in between. Americans, he said, were not hauled out in front of firing squads, or sent to Siberia, or involved in high dramas staged in baronial grandeur. Their existences were, in a favorite word, "commonplace." He felt the charm and the pathos of ordinary people—the world of the summer boardinghouse, the straw-hatted strangers on a ferryboat, the blurred and unknown yet intimately familiar personages in somebody else's snapshot. For

Howells as for Eakins, the camera held powerful truths. It caught people unawares, unposed, anonymous yet profoundly real. He tried to catch this random, unheroic, tender truth in his fiction—as Whitman at his best had, so to speak, taken Kodak pictures of a myriad, mysteriously evocative American scenes.

Howells had to grapple with two perplexing difficulties. One was that little by little he lost confidence in the unfolding of America's national life. The Haymarket "massacre" of 1886 was a bad jar for him. No longer able to believe that the United States was spared the cruelties of Europe, he began to try to incorporate strikes, violence, and misery in his stories. He was a gentle man, who sought a way out in utopian fiction. Others had preceded him, especially Edward Bellamy, the author of *Looking Backward: 2000–1887* (1888). Another glimpse of the future, this time a bleak one, was offered in *Caesar's Column* (1891), a novel by Ignatius Donnelly. Howells's first contribution to fantasy fiction, *A Traveler from Altruria* (1894), exposed contemporary America to the gentle probing of a character on a visit from an imaginary, ideal country—the sort of country the United States ought to be, and could be if it tried hard enough.

The second difficulty for Howells was that his own brand of realism began to seem dated and timid, even though he gave generous encouragement to the new wave of writers. Unlike his friend Twain, whose humor became steadily more barbed and despondent, Howells clung to an essential faith in American decency. He could not bring himself to explore the underside of human nature. By the 1890s, however, realism for such writers as Hamlin Garland, Stephen Crane, Frank Norris, and Theodore Dreiser entailed the recognition that people were driven by forces—sex, fear, greed, social pressure, economic necessity—over which they had little or no control. Crane's *Maggie* (1893) sketched the short unhappy life of a prostitute. It tried, he said, to "show that environment is a tremendous thing . . . , and frequently shapes lives regardless." His brilliant Civil War novel *The Red Badge of Courage* (1895) suggested that combat was a nightmare, and heroism in battle a chancy business. *McTeague* (1899), by Norris, depicts the helpless slide of the "hero" into poverty, murder, and his own gruesome death. Norris's *The Octopus* (1901) describes the plight of California wheat farmers in the tentacles of a railroad which ruthlessly imposes its terms upon them. Dreiser's *Sister Carrie* (1900) is a country girl who comes to Chicago and inevitably, since she is both poor and pretty, allows herself to be kept by a couple of men. "We suffer for our temperaments," Dreiser subsequently declared, "which we did not make, and for our weaknesses and lacks, which are no part of our willing or doing." The message of such "naturalistic" fiction, consciously or unconsciously influenced by Darwinism, was that men and women are victims of circumstance. Virtue and vice were old-fashioned ideas with little relevance to the "real" world. Mark Twain came near to saying the same thing in such later writings as *The Tragedy of Pudd'nhead Wilson* (1894) and *The Man that Corrupted Hadleyburg* (1900).

Howells and James never reached so gloomy a conclusion. Nor did the educated American public who followed serial fiction in *Scribner's, Century, Harper's,* and other prominent magazines. Nor were Crane and Norris entirely converted to naturalism. Both were fascinated by travel, color, adventure. Slum conditions, or indeed life on the farm, were, they conceded, drably harsh. But life also contained epic drama, gorgeous and exotic moments—in a word, romance. Realism as they sometimes envisaged it—Dreiser and the young writer Jack London agreed—was not an affair of trivial, low-key incidents, but something big, powerful, vital. A glance at the magazines of the era brings out this duality. Many of the novels and short stories in them could be called realistic. They included "local-color" vignettes, the use of dialect, an almost photographic fidelity in description, and plots that deliberately avoided sentimentality. Many other contributions, however, emphasized nostalgia, chivalry, and gracious living. If realism signified having one's nose

Simple, everyday aspects of American life appealed to William Dean Howells. This photograph typifies the commonplace experience of ordinary people, which Howells reflected in his writing.

Courtesy of New York State Historical Association, Cooperstown

rubbed in unpleasantness, the majority of Americans preferred such books as Thomas Nelson Page's *In Ole Virginia* (1887), Frances Hodgson Burnett's *Little Lord Fauntleroy* (1886), Mark Twain's unexpectedly reverent *Joan of Arc* (1896), and Charles Major's *When Knighthood Was in Flower* (1898). Profound shifts in American thought and taste were in the making. The best minds and talents of the Gilded Age had honestly tried to map their era according to their own lights. There was still, they knew, a long way to go; and there was a bewildering quantity of rival recommendations for the route to be followed.

"There was things which he stretched, but mainly he told the truth." This extract from Huckleberry Finn *is, in fact, an exceedingly apt description of its author's literary approach. Mark Twain (above) was renowned for his subtle weavings of deadpan humor with wild exaggeration. The* Personal Recollections of Joan of Arc *(1896) was considered by Twain to be his best work; his critics took the opposite view. Right: This illustration appeared in a later edition of* Joan of Arc.

Chapter 5

THE IMPACT OF CHANGE

Industrialism and the growth of the city went hand in hand. But the new jobs and the wide range of entertainment in urban areas were accompanied by slums, crime, fire hazards, and epidemics. Solutions were proposed for many of these problems; some of them worked and some did not, but the rush to the cities could not be halted. In rural areas, meanwhile, farmers were undergoing hard times. Skyrocketing costs for supplies and for transportation of produce, coupled with low prices in the marketplace, resulted in lean years for many. Farmers saw their way of life eroded and began to fight back through political action; the climax was the election of 1896.

The Bright Lights of the City

In America as in England and Europe, the growth of industry meant the growth of cities. The city was the birthplace and fabricator of the ingenious machines that revolutionized the economy. It was the home of the creative arts and the practical sciences that flourished in the latter part of the century. It supplied the principal forum for the political contests which commenced with a scramble for spoils and ended with a search for civic reform. As the workshop for labor, it served as the great magnet drawing immigrants to America. But most characteristic of all, its bright lights attracted an increasing influx of rural and small-town residents who joined in transforming America from an agrarian into an industrial nation.

The lure of the city did not displace the pull of the West until the 1890s, but even in the 1870s it was playing a dominant role in the westward movement. California was already in that decade the fifth most urbanized state, and by the turn of the century Colorado and Washington would also rank among the top fifteen in percentage of urban dwellers. San Francisco had attained and continued to hold tenth place in size among the nation's cities, and enjoyed a higher rating for its cosmopolitan culture. Few cities demonstrated more vividly than the always enchanting port at the Golden Gate that the lure of the city was not exclusively industrial or even economic.

The urbanization movement was shared by much of the Western world, but America experienced a unique version of the trend. Total urban growth exceeded the rural gains for the first time in the 1860s and then progressively widened its lead. The rate of acceleration was especially remarkable since, as a new land, America was experiencing a large rural population growth as well. Its high rate of urbanization reflected the huge influx of immigrants, most of whom settled in the cities. The resulting diversity of population, coupled with the wide geographic diffusion of urban sites, produced a cultural hotchpotch that added to the problems as well as to the opportunities and the fascination of American cities.

Yet the tumultuous growth of the cities, particularly of the forty that exceeded 100,000 by 1900, also demonstrated the skill of local promoters in developing their commercial and industrial potentialities. Only Washington, the national capital, prospered without an economic base. Other towns had to compensate for poor geographical locations or deficient natural assets. Some, like Kansas City, exerted themselves to provide railroads or other man-made arteries of trade. Other towns, such as Paterson, New Jersey, encouraged the development of factories. Still others exploited their natural resources, as in the case of Scranton, Pennsylvania, with its rich anthracite deposits. In a few instances the site proved decisive, as with Minneapolis, the flour-milling center located at the great falls of the Mississippi and in the heart of Minnesota, a wheat-growing state. Elsewhere local entrepreneurs had to choose their specialties, often by trial and error. Rochester was an example of a city which had to change its ways with the times. In its early days it had been a flour-milling center; but with the push west and the subsequent cultivation of midwestern wheat, Rochester's flour industry grew obsolete. Business leaders of the city responded by basing its survival on the skills of a stream of newcomers who manned the clothing, shoe, and technical industries. No industrial city could rival the geographical advantages of Pittsburgh, situated as it was in the midst of coal and iron fields and at a river and rail junction of exceptional accessibility. "This is the domain of Vulcan, not of Pluto," declared Willard Glazier, a British traveler, as he viewed its blazing furnaces on a balmy night in the fall of 1882.

Few cities were as spectacularly lit up as Pittsburgh on such nights, but growth in size and technology had made it necessary and opportune for many to light their streets and public places as never before. The gas lights that had made their appearance in a score of cities in pre-Civil War days now spread rapidly to the great

The dazzling variety of entertainments in the cities was a constant lure to country dwellers. Burlesque, roller skating, and melodrama were three popular diversions in the "Gay Nineties."

majority of cities. They provided lighted Main Streets that attracted throngs of strollers on Saturday nights and at the same time promoted a new sense of community. The new, more widely shared night life spilled over into dance halls, roller-skating rinks, and popular theaters, as well as into the more formal lecture and music halls. These and other evening functions received a new impetus with the arrival of electric lights in the 1880s and 1890s. And the pull of the bright lights, which a few years before had brought streams of urban residents downtown, now

subdividers vied with building associations in the development of new tracts, generally with little municipal guidance. But the need to retain easy access to the city and the desire to share in its services helped to maintain a semblance of order in urban expansion.

Construction activities within the older sections of the cities were similarly incessant—and even more chaotic. Most of the original structures in the inner-city districts had long since given way to more substantial buildings, some of them third or fourth generation. On the principal

The construction of streetcar lines caused temporary disruption of traffic, as this 1891 photograph of New York's Union Square suggests. But once completed, they radically improved travel within cities.

attracted excursion trains full of distant villagers and farmers eager to visit the stores, theaters, and hot spots of the cities.

Many of the visitors, particularly the young men and women, found jobs and homes in the cities. The search for homes stimulated the conversion of old mansions into rooming houses, and of lofts over stores and shops into flats or in some cases into slum dormitories. The demand for new houses brought a rush of activity every spring and summer on the outskirts of most cities. Speculative

downtown streets of many cities, brick or stone or cast-iron fronts, rising to four or five stories in solid phalanx, provided a rigid mold for a congested business district. Banks, stores, and specialty shops vied for the favored locations. Churches, schools, and factories, pushed out of these central districts, found lodgment on radial avenues.

Hacks and omnibuses supplemented pedestrian movement, but as early as the 1850s these had begun to give way in a few large cities to horsecar lines. By 1880 local companies had laid tracks and were providing service in all cities of 50,000 or more. New York and Philadelphia had previously built commuter lines equipped with steam trains to link suburbs and outer sections with the center of the city. By 1890 ten other cities annually reported over 5 million commuters. San Francisco successfully constructed a cable line to haul cars up and down its famous Nob Hill in 1872, and Chicago quickly adopted this efficient but costly method of transit in its expanding business districts. Soon forty other cities, eager to reduce the congestion—and droppings—created by thousands of horses in their busy streets, also installed cable-car lines. In the 1890s Chicago and Boston adopted New York's earlier policy of building elevated rail lines for the steam-driven commuter trains.

The great breakthrough came in the mid-1880s when

huge department stores to supply all a shopper's needs under one roof.

As pressure mounted for the remodeling of old districts to accommodate their increased densities, some property owners added new floors to old structures. Others constructed new and taller buildings. The development of the passenger elevator in these decades, first operated by hydraulic power or steam and finally in the late eighties by electricity, greatly spurred the upward extension of office buildings. New York had experimented in the 1850s

Museum of the City of New York

Thomas A. Edison among others perfected the electric motor. Several cities installed experimental lines, and in 1888 Richmond, Virginia, operated the first successful trolley service on one of its principal streets. By the end of the first decade of the twentieth century over 900 companies were operating some 48,000 cars along a total of 15,000 miles of track, greatly easing movement within most American cities.

These developments had many repercussions. Speedier transit increased the efficiency of business transactions and drew larger numbers of workers and shoppers into the central districts. Some enterprising merchants expanded their lines and, following the earlier lead of Alexander Stewart in New York, John Wanamaker in Philadelphia, and Marshall Field in Chicago, developed

Not only was the elevated railway a major advance in commuter transportation: it added a new visual drama to the cities. W. Louis Sonntag, Jr executed this oil The Bowery at Night *in 1895.*

with the use of cast-iron fronts and interior piers, and by the 1860s and 1870s other cities were following New York's lead. At the same time Chicago was introducing iron piers as reinforcements in the outer walls. Encouraged by the development of fireproofing techniques and pressed by the mounting densities in its central district, venturesome Chicago architects, led by William Jenney and Louis Sullivan, designed and erected the first skyscrapers in the mid-1880s. The Chicago pattern, consisting of a metal skeleton soaring ten or more stories high, sheathed in brick or masonry walls with spacious windows set in cast-iron bays on frames, created a new structural model to which Sullivan gave a fresh architectural grace. St Louis and St Paul in the Midwest, and New York and other cities in the East hastened to construct two or more skyscrapers each in the early 1890s. In effect these could be seen as vertical streets, added to relieve the density at congested corners for part of the day, but increasing it tremendously at noontime and evening breaks.

Other technological breakthroughs contributed to the success of the skyscrapers and to the development of cities in general. Improvements in the design and manufacture of lead and iron piping had made it possible to distribute water and to collect sewage. Most cities had already provided these services by the 1880s, so that all skyscrapers were able to install sanitary facilities on every floor. In similar fashion, improvements in furnaces and ducts made it possible to supply central heating to all rooms of large office and commercial blocks. Electric lighting had also just become available as these buildings took shape. Moreover the telephone, perfected in the 1870s and coinciding with the exhibition at the Philadelphia Centennial (1876), had attracted quick acceptance. Business leaders in numerous cities had hastily organized 148 telephone companies, which served 48,000 subscribers chiefly in the central districts by 1880. Although some companies failed and others merged with stronger rivals, the number of subscribers increased fivefold in the 1880s. Each office in the new skyscrapers had one or more telephones connecting it with scattered firms, thus reducing their dependence on the still slow-moving elevators.

Many cities had assumed the tasks of supplying water and collecting sewage, at least in substantially built-up areas, before or shortly after the Civil War. Most of the others did so when the great fires in Boston (1872) and Chicago (1871) and the yellow fever epidemic (1878) in Memphis demonstrated the folly of neglecting these services. In Rochester, Daniel Powers, owner of the largest commercial block, suddenly resigned from the tax league. He left the league because it had maintained that the city could not afford a waterworks. He then became chairman of a citizens' committee, formed while the Chicago fire was still raging, to demand the immediate construction of not just one, but two waterworks.

The ravages of cholera in earlier years had prompted New York, on the threat of a new epidemic in 1866, to create a metropolitan board of health with authority to enforce sanitary regulations. Other cities followed, and

The Chicago fire of October 8, 1871, destroyed 2,000 acres of the city's heartland. Until then an overgrown frontier town, Chicago was rebuilt in a manner befitting a metropolis.

The density of urban populations was always most apparent in the tenements. At the time this photograph of Harlem was taken (1900), the population of New York exceeded 3.4 million.

some appointed physicians rather than politicians as many had done in previous emergencies. Some gave heed to the pleas of their boards for adequate water supplies and for the prompt removal of garbage and human waste. The latter concern dwindled as the distribution of running water permitted the installation of inside toilets even in the poorer districts. Nevertheless, many cities continued to rely on surface drains and neighboring streams to remove their discharge. But when Memphis, reeling from a toll of 5,000 deaths from yellow fever in 1878, hastened to lay several miles of sanitary sewers, other cities gave the problem closer attention. Boston had been alarmed the year before to hear its inner harbor described by health authorities as "a vast cesspool." Chicago was endeavoring to reverse the flow of the Chicago River in order to carry its foul discharge off to the distant Mississippi River. This measure would thereby save Lake Michigan as its water supply. Boston decided to discharge its sewage into the outer bay where the tides would remove it. The town of Lawrence, Massachusetts, on the Merrimack, suffering from industrial congestion,

began to experiment with a new sand filter to safeguard the region's ecology. In 1888 Providence, Rhode Island, established the world's first municipal bacteriological laboratory.

New York's health board had uncovered another sanitary hazard in the congested slum districts in its older quarters. The discovery of thousands of poor persons huddled in dilapidated structures, often with one or more families to a room, alerted civic leaders to the need for regulation. When the first tenement house law of 1867 proved inadequate, the city secured a revision twelve years later which required a window in every room and other minimal health provisions. A contest for the most economical plans conforming to these regulations produced a design for a series of small apartments to be constructed in tiers on New York's deep but narrow lots. The four- and five-story structures with a dumbbell-shaped ground plan spread rapidly and extensively over Manhattan. Adding to an already crowded city and creating a density unrivaled elsewhere, the new tenements boosted the passenger totals on the four elevated railway lines that served the area to an annual 200 million by the early 1890s. Furthermore they developed unparalleled demands for civic and domestic services that exceeded the capacities of officials and merchants alike.

Boston had likewise discovered the presence of nascent

slums in the 1870s. It had adopted building codes that allowed for construction of four-story three-deckers, which spread over South Boston and into some of the new streetcar suburbs of the 1880s and 1890s. By filling in Back Bay and expanding onto and beyond it, Boston somewhat relieved the congestion in its old South End and West End. A similar expansion in Philadelphia and Chicago took the pressure off their older districts. These and other rapidly growing cities—St Louis, Cleveland, and San Francisco among them—adopted new building codes. Such cities concerned themselves more directly with the fire hazard than with the housing problem. Nonetheless citizen housing committees were forming in several places.

The water mains and hydrants which were penetrating into all sections of the city greatly simplified the task of the firemen. Unfortunately the hand pumps of the volunteer companies proved ineffective against fires above the third story, and as a result of this most cities required at least one or two of the new steamers. These appeared for the first time in the late 1860s, but were much too costly to be entrusted to volunteers. As cities acquired them they created central fire departments, and employed full-time firemen to run the engine companies and tend the horses required to pull the engines. By the 1880s most large cities had numerous engine companies, and the dashing response they made at the sound of the fire alarm

added new drama to the urban scene. Assisted by volunteer companies equipped with hook-and-ladder trucks, and in coastal towns by steam fire boats, the fire departments represented a major civic investment. But the boosting of fire insurance rates in negligent cities increased the pressure for effective precautions. Several cities also installed fire-alarm telegraph systems to speed up action.

Equally if not more important were the police departments. Eight cities had appointed police chiefs and created small departments of uniformed police by the mid-1860s, and all the major cities quickly fell into line. As the number of police officers multiplied, generally at a faster rate than the city's population, they acquired additional functions.

The crime ratios were mounting, particularly in such rapidly growing cities as Chicago and San Francisco. Frequent outbreaks of violence in industrial cities during periods of economic crisis, and in depressed neighborhoods undergoing ethnic transition, taxed the abilities of the police to maintain order. Recurrent demands for the enforcement of laws against gambling and vice and for

Little boys gape and residents stare as a policeman removes a drunkard from New York's Mulberry Bend. A squalid and depressed area, the "Bend" had a consistently high incidence of crime.

THE IMPACT OF CHANGE

the adoption of ordinances designed to preserve a quiet Sabbath prompted successive police chiefs to stage dramatic drives for law and order. In many cities the contest for police control became a major political issue, and the charges and countercharges of corruption frequently weakened their morale. But the development of specialized detective forces, the provision of police telephones, the creation in some of the larger metropolises of squads of mounted officers to control crowds, and in the 1890s of bicycle squads to apprehend reckless or speeding ''scorchers,''—all of these innovations helped to maintain the vitality of the police function.

Several of the leading cities developed another major contingent of municipal employees—the sanitation workers. As the towns grew, the old practice of relying on

Overcrowded living conditions increased fire hazards and disease in the nation's larger cities. Left: A horse-drawn steam engine creates a spectacular sight as it races to the scene of a fire. Below: This photograph, taken in the 1890s, depicts garbage collection in New York's garment district.

private garbage collectors brought frequent crises, especially in extremely hot or bitterly cold weather. At the earnest behest of their health boards, numerous cities assumed the task of garbage collection and disposal and sometimes the removal of other refuse as well. Several followed Philadelphia's example and built incinerators or reduction plants, although the returns from the by-products proved minimal. To improve the generally low morale of his force, Colonel George E. Waring in New York dressed his men in white and in 1896 staged the first public parade of ''White Wings'' on lower Broadway. Some cities used the drivers and teams of the collection carts to operate sweepers to clean the streets in spring and fall. In the summer they were used to haul sprinklers to keep down the dust on macadamized boulevards. A few cities in the Northeast began to employ the same teams to plow the snow from their main business streets in winter months. Most cities, however, continued to rely on a change in weather to solve these problems.

The problems of maintaining the city streets changed with the weather, but they did not go away. The traditional macadam improvement with crushed stone

Clothed in a uniform designed to lend dignity to his task, a member of the "White Wings," New York's Department of Street Cleaners, poses for the camera at 46th Street and Sixth Avenue in 1894.

proved unsuitable for heavy traffic, and after 1869 numerous cities followed New York's lead of paving its principal streets with granite blocks. Some cities, lacking suitable quarries, used wooden blocks; others experimented with brick pavements. Washington made the first extensive use of asphalt in 1882, which Buffalo and several other cities quickly adopted. As the demand exceeded the supply, prices soared and several cities endeavored to break the monopoly control over its production.

A more common problem with street maintenance was the timing of desired improvements. Many of the older city streets were macadamized before the laying of water mains, sanitary sewers, and gas lines was undertaken. Frequently these operations were not carefully coordinated so that the pavement was periodically dis-

rupted and soon had to be replaced. The installation of street lights and the erection of telephone and electric poles and wires further complicated the maintenance problem. To free its busy streets of festoons of wires, New York began in 1889 to place them in underground conduits. Many cities followed this lead, which immediately resulted in another franchise dispute.

Most American cities relied on private companies to build and operate their gas, electric, telephone, and transit systems. So eager were they in most cases for these services that generous franchises were awarded, extending in many cases for three or more decades. Few of the franchises were exclusive, for the cities relied on competition to maintain reasonable rates and services. This, however, soon proved inefficient both for the city and for the companies. The trend everywhere was towards exclusive franchises or a division of territory, plus more specific requirements as to service and charges. Inevitably, the pressure for favorable franchises drew local politicians into questionable deals that stirred popular demands for reform.

Urban political contests frequently focused on questions of economy, law enforcement, and services. And the public service that generally proved most costly was education, which brought it repeatedly into politics. The cities had been the first to provide free public schools in the 1840s, and many had since achieved city-wide systems under the direction of elected boards of education and administrative superintendents. These had adopted the graded system and increased the number of subjects covered to include elementary science and history as well as grammar and the traditional three Rs. And they had progressively added new grades, extending public instruction down into the kindergarten years and up into the high school level in order to prepare all students to participate in the complex urban society. Under the leadership of urban teacher-training programs, they developed new educational techniques, substituting "learning by doing," as John Dewey conceived it, for much routine memory work. They pressed for compulsory attendance laws, achieving their adoption in twenty-six states by 1890. But enforcement was lax, and a survey of seventeen cities already covered by such laws a decade before found only eight with an attendance of at least half of those eligible.

Yet the urban efforts and expectations in respect to the public schools were so high that the results often proved disappointing. In 1893 the depression put many young men out of work. Civic leaders striving to place them in other jobs became indignant over the poor

Winter in northern cities posed a unique problem for city administrators. This view of New Street, near Wall Street, shows the paralysis visited on New York by the Blizzard of '88.

education they had received. In Rochester and several other cities, discovering that the appointment of teachers had been a part of the spoils system, reformers led a campaign to free the schools from political control. In their search for support they learned of the existence of similar groups in other cities. They sent delegates to the annual Good Government Conferences that met in Philadelphia, Minneapolis, and other cities in the mid-1890s. There the educational reformers rubbed shoulders with the opponents of vice and corruption, with the advocates of parks and public health measures, as well as with members of tax conscious groups. Together they developed a plan for the organization of good government clubs in the wards and precincts of each alert city. Soon these various local leagues were challenging the dominant party's control in a dozen cities. In Chicago the Municipal Voters' League engaged a paid executive to direct the campaign, but volunteers proved effective in most cities. In Rochester, for example, they not only freed the schools from politics but developed a system that increasingly served the great majority of eligible children, including many from immigrant families; they also opened evening classes for adults eager to learn English, civics, or a basic mechanical skill.

The Arena of Urban Reform

As the civic reformers won scattered victories, sometimes on single issues, they frequently broadened their platforms to include an upgrading of municipal services generally. In prosperous times these improvement drives stirred little controversy, and the partisan bosses were often ready and eager to endorse and absorb the reform programs. The good government movement would have quickly lost its force had it not been for the struggle in city after city over the grant of utility franchises. Where the civic reformers sided with business groups eager to promote a new utility at any cost, champions of the public interest, such as Tom Johnson in Cleveland, arose to combat them. But when the civic reformers rallied to check a fradulent bid for a lucrative franchise, as they did at Chicago when they blocked a railroad grab by Charles T. Yerkes in 1900, their vitality was renewed.

The staging of the Columbian Exposition at Chicago (1893), led to a resurgence of the city's vitality. The fair's spectacular success created a wide interest in city planning, public parks, and civic improvements generally. The increasing charm of Central Park in New York had brought its designer, Frederick Law Olmsted, numerous commissions from other cities. In Boston he laid out the Fenway Park System, and in Chicago he not only prepared the landscape design for the great fair but also planned the idyllic Riverside suburb. The new interest in

planning inspired by the exposition focused on the development of downtown civic plazas as in Cleveland, on the proper location and landscaping of public buildings as in Washington, and on the development of park systems and suburban boulevards as in Kansas City, Detroit, and Chicago.

Yet the urban planners of the 1880s and 1890s were still working in two dimensions. They failed to take account of the rising skyscrapers, except in a few cases where they placed limits on their heights. But the construction of skyscrapers had been checked by the depression, and a more immediate need was for attention to the social dimensions of urban life. The unemployment and destitution present in many districts of the larger cities called for more than educational reforms. First, however, it was necessary to inform the average citizen of the plight of his less fortunate neighbors. In vivid newspaper articles, later assembled in a moving account of *How the Other Half Lives,* Jacob Riis alerted thousands of readers to conditions in the slums.

Of course the problems of the underprivileged were not new, nor were they born of the depression of the 1890s. Many were deeply rooted in the hectic growth of the cities, particularly the great ports where poor newcomers congregated. The earlier depression of the mid-1870s had aggravated their difficulties, prompting the creation of relief agencies in New York, Philadelphia, and Boston. A similar move in Buffalo had resulted in the establishment of the first Charity Organization Society to supervise the administration of private relief funds. This effort to assure adequate coverage, and yet to check the development of pauperism, spread quickly to other cities. A resurgent temperance campaign diverted evangelical groups in many cities to a moralistic attack on the saloon as the principal cause of poverty. But the charity organization movement persisted, and more than thirty of the leading cities had charity organization societies by the late 1880s.

Settlement Houses and the Social Gospel

While these bodies helped to promote cooperation between the relief programs, charitable homes, and other institutions of the various denominations, they touched only the fringes of the problem. A new approach by a group of settlement houses made a more penetrating attack on poverty. The settlement houses were established in slum districts by groups of dedicated volunteers who took up residence there and shared some of the hardships of the blighted districts. The volunteers sought to win the confidence and cooperation of the poor in the development of welfare and cultural programs. Residents of these houses, headed by Jane Addams in Chicago, Lillian D.

Wald in New York, and Robert A. Woods in Boston, acquired the experience that made them the leaders of the new profession of social workers. Soon their surveys and reports substantiated many of the journalistic reports of Riis and his successors. In addition they attracted the interest of urban universities, prompting them to staff the settlement houses with their own graduate students.

Religious groups had from the beginning made major contributions to urban charities. In the 1860s denominational rivalries had prompted the establishment of separate homes and other services. Although the depression of the 1870s inspired efforts at cooperation among the sects, resurgent ethnic rivalries reestablished old differences. The depression of the 1890s, which transformed the flagging societies for organized charity into united charities, promoted cooperation. But it soon became apparent to settlement house residents and to clergymen that the diversity was not so much doctrinal as cultural and that a new dimension of understanding was required to achieve a mutual accord.

Some of the liberal clergymen accepted posts in the Protestant churches of the inner city. These churches were surrounded now by newcomers from abroad whose cultural traditions were as foreign as their religious heritage, but whose poverty and humanity called for compassionate friendship. Recognizing that the Christian ministry had a responsibility for the welfare of men and women in this world, farsighted clerics developed a social gospel that rose above Protestant, Catholic, and Jewish rivalries, a doctrine that surmounted many traditional mores as well. Thus Walter Rauschenbusch, among other spokesmen for Social Christianity, came to see that the saloon was the only club, indeed the only living room, for many poor workingmen crowded in wretched dormitory lofts. Instead of enforcing the Sabbath closing ordinance, the city, Rauschenbusch declared, should develop its parks and recreational facilities and provide programs on Sundays to offer the slum-dweller wholesome alternatives. He also urged merchants and industrialists to pay their workers enough to enable them to marry and raise families. He further proposed that they join with other firms in granting half the day off on Saturdays.

Advocates of the social gospel comprised only a minority even in the urban churches, most of which continued to serve their own congregations, often following them, as the city expanded, into the suburbs. The Catholic churches, which now outnumbered all Protestant denominations in many cities, both in members and in attendance, were less inclined to move their parishes. Nevertheless some ethnic newcomers desired and finally secured Catholic churches with priests who spoke their native tongues. Similarly the Jews established their own synagogues, liberal or orthodox in accord with their origins, sometimes remodeling an abandoned

Protestant edifice to fit their needs. New urban-centered sects, notably the Christian Scientists, who endeavored to solve their health problems by a renewal of faith, and a new breed of evangelists, led on the one hand by Dwight L. Moody and Ira D. Sankey and on the other by William Booth of the Salvation Army, attracted large followings throughout the country partly through the dramatic character of their appeals.

Leisure Activities and Mass Entertainment

Cities fostered novelty and excitement in many fields. The numerous local baseball clubs formed in every city after the Civil War soon engendered an inter-city rivalry that prompted a consolidation of forces in each town. Inspired by the success of the Red Stockings of Cincinnati, the new local clubs supported professional teams, eight of which joined to form the National League in 1876. Its regulations, followed by several regional leagues, helped to standardize the game and promote exciting contests that required increasingly larger ball parks and grandstands. Horse racing attracted similar spectator support in some cities. At least a dozen saw the development by local driving clubs of spacious race tracks where contestants from scattered stables gathered for week-long racing seasons once or twice a year. Local and visiting gamblers enjoyed a freer hand at these contests than at the ball games, from which they were generally excluded. Numerous other sports found an eager welcome in the cities and enlisted a wider participation within limited circles—tennis and especially golf among the more affluent, rowing clubs in river towns and yacht clubs at lake and ocean port cities. The perfection of the safety bicycle resulted in the formation in the late 1880s and 1890s of hundreds of cycle clubs. To remove the dangerous "scorchers" from the principal streets and sidewalks, numerous cities supported drives for sidepaths and for the improvement of highways to nearby picnic groves and commercial resorts. The increasing rush in the summer to beaches and other watering places demonstrated the popularity of public bathing—despite the continued restraints on swimwear. The steaming city streets prompted middle-class citizens to take annual vacations at private cottages or summer hotels in lake or mountain resorts.

In winter months some favored urbanites took trips abroad, but most found an escape from their daily concerns by a visit to one of the local theaters or concert halls. The old hostility to theaters disappeared and they found a place in every city and all towns of any size. The performers of Shakespearean and other classical plays shared the stage with troupes presenting American dramatists, some of whom tackled urban topics. Generally,

Americans in the late nineteenth century enjoyed a variety of leisure pursuits. Tennis, introduced from England, appealed to both sexes. Baseball was an exclusively amateur game in 1866, when the lithograph below appeared. The Chicago Jockey & Trotting Club offered free oats to participating horses. Bathing was popular—and so were comic sketches of life by the seaside. Opposite bottom: An enthusiastic crowd watches John L. Sullivan (on the left) retain his world heavyweight crown against Jake Kilrain in 1889.

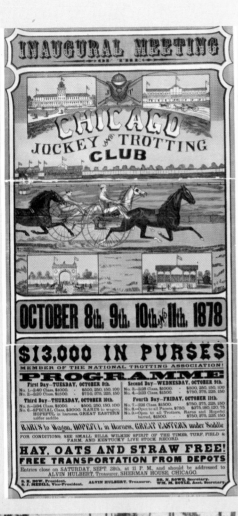

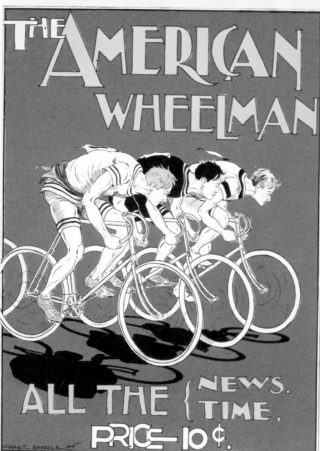

Cycling in 1896 was a $60 million business: the sport attracted both men and women. Right: Frances Willard, president of the Women's Christian Temperance Union, learns to ride with the help of three friends. Below right: The champion waves his hat after the finish of the New York Evening Telegram Parade. Below: Derby-hatted crowds await the start of the Martin Road Race in Buffalo on Memorial Day, 1894. To keep abreast of latest innovations, enthusiasts pored over a host of cycling magazines, of which the American Wheelman (below left) was one. Left: Touring cyclists pose with their "ordinaries" outside Tallahassee.

Courtesy National Women's Christian Temperance Union

Museum of the City of New York

drama was designed to amuse audiences whose memories reached back to rural scenes. Such plays appealed especially to villagers on a shopping trip to the city, while the new vaudeville shows and "leg shows" supplied an enticement available only in major cities. The popularity of Gilbert and Sullivan operettas in the 1880s and 1890s pushed the perennial revivals of *Uncle Tom's Cabin* into the small-town theaters. In half a dozen cities, music hall performers encouraged their leaders to establish professional symphony orchestras, and to develop orchestral societies which appeared in a dozen more before the turn of the century.

If the bright lights of the theaters and concert halls

St Louis Post-Dispatch

The Bettmann Archive

Editor of the New York World, *Joseph Pulitzer (left) vied with William Randolph Hearst (right) of the New York* Journal *for increased circulation in a spectacular match of one-upmanship. The sensational reporting used by both papers came to be known as yellow journalism. Hearst won the contest and Pulitzer resumed his earlier dedication to serious and noteworthy journalism.*

added to the lure of the cities, the attraction of their galleries and academies was also impressive. Privately supported art galleries, such as the one Daniel Powers opened on the fifth floor of his commercial block in Rochester, New York, commanded the attention of all self-respecting visitors in an age when trips to Europe were still reserved for the favored few. Art clubs, enrolling some who had studied abroad, vied in interest with the scientific academies. These afforded opportunities for young and old students of geology, botany, astronomy, and numerous other subjects to exhibit collections and read papers that sometimes led to creative careers in science or literature. Many of the popular academies soon became associated with the libraries which made their appearance in most cities in these decades. Established in many cases by associations or

generous patrons, they increasingly won at least a measure of public support. In the larger cities branch libraries extended their services into residential neighborhoods. As their collections mounted, the problem of locating specific books increased. A classification system developed by Melvin Dewey—in time for display at the Centennial in Philadelphia—attracted immediate acceptance and soon made the library resources of American cities more accessible than those of any other country.

But for most readers the daily newspaper and perhaps a favorite periodical sufficed. No magazine rivaled the continued success of *Harper's Monthly* and *Harper's Weekly*, but at least fifty of the numerous journals that appeared more or less briefly in one city or another achieved a regional or national circulation and several boasted a distribution of 100,000 or more by 1900. The daily newspapers enjoyed a much wider readership. With at least three competing fiercely in every city of 50,000 or more, and with foreign language papers serving the ethnic districts, nearly every viewpoint found expression. As these papers grew in size from eight to sixteen to twenty-four or more pages, they added extended excerpts from sermons and lectures. In addition they included columns on the theater, sports events, the police court, and the world of society. By reporting fires, accidents, and institutional events they enhanced their service as community diaries, while their editorial comments reflected at least one side of current political and social controversies. Aside from the great metropolitan journals, such as Charles A. Dana's New York *Sun* and Joseph Pulitzer's New York *World,* the daily papers gave minimal coverage of national news except at election time or during a period of crisis. The development of syndicated columns and of the Associated Press partly corrected this deficiency in leading local papers. As the wood cuts and copper engravings, first used to enliven the advertisements, spilled over into the text, political cartoons appeared, as did the first comic strips.

But the real explosion occurred when Randolph Hearst challenged Pulitzer's *World* with the new sensational techniques he had developed on the San Francisco *Examiner.* His dramatic struggle to gain sole publishing rights on "The Yellow Kid" comic strip for the New York *Morning Journal* from the *World,* and their sensational reporting of the dispute with Spain over Cuba, not only gave birth to the new term "yellow journalism" but forced the reluctant McKinley into a declaration of war. It so clearly demonstrated the power of the press that newspapers everywhere assumed a new and more aggressive posture. No longer content to serve as recording diaries, they took their place on the platform in the glare of the newly invented spot lights. They became the champions of both the heterogeneity and the lure of the city.

The Johnstown Flood

"The Historic Catastrophe," proclaimed the Boston *Post*. "TEN THOUSAND DEAD," declared the New York *World*. "The most extraordinary calamity of the age," claimed *Frank Leslie's Illustrated Newspaper*. Soon after reports reached the press offices that a small Pennsylvania iron town had been wracked by flood, the newspapers began trying to outdo each other with exaggerated claims of carnage and destruction.

The story of the Johnstown flood stems from events seventeen years before the incident. In 1872 a group of wealthy Pittsburgh men began to build a sporting club. The site, South Fork, was a lush mountain spot fourteen miles east of Johnstown. At one time, there had been a man-made lake at South Fork, but that had effectively disappeared when an earth dam holding it back gave way during a flood in 1862. (Fortunately the damage was slight.) In order to provide fishing and sailing for its members, the club decided to refill the lake. But instead of properly reconstructing the dam, the club simply patched it up.

On the evening of Memorial Day 1889, the rain started. It poured down relentlessly and by morning the Stony Creek and Conemaugh River (which converged in Johnstown) were running very high. Behind the dam itself, the water was rising a foot an hour.

At three o'clock in the afternoon of May 31, 1889, the dam collapsed in the center, spilling its 20 million tons of water onto Johnstown. "It just seemed like a mountain coming," said one survivor. At first there was so much debris caught up in the torrent that the water underneath— traveling at some stages at forty miles per hour—could not be seen. As soon as they were struck by the onslaught, men, women, and children, livestock, houses, railway cars—all joined the surge.

In the days following the flood, newspapers launched zealous pleas of help for the flood victims. The response brought overwhelming amounts of clothing, money, food, medical supplies —even coffins and nails. Reporting on the aftermath, a correspondent from the New York *Daily Graphic* wrote,

"It is a scene which blanches the faces of strong men, and in its multiplying horror is almost beyond description."

One aspect journalists failed to mention was who in fact belonged to the club; Andrew Carnegie, Henry Clay Frick, and Andrew W. Mellon were prominent club members. Suits were filed against the club. In addition to the loss of 2,209 lives (as opposed to the 10,000 reported by the *World*), property worth $17 million had been destroyed. Although public opinion concurred that the club's makeshift repairs were responsible for the dam's collapse and the subsequent damage, this view did not gain the sympathy of judges. Not one cent was awarded to the claimants.

In the years to follow, Johnstown would feature in coarse jokes. One example was the common barroom notice which read: "Please don't spit on the floor. Remember the Johnstown flood."

Lurid and often false newspaper reports of the Johnstown disaster were sometimes accompanied by imaginative artists' impressions. In reality, few Johnstown residents were wearing night clothes when the flood struck in the afternoon.

Kurz & Allison, 1890

Wealth Against Commonwealth

Eldorado, Kansas, was a country town of 2,500 people in 1890. Thomas Benton Murdock, editor and sole proprietor of the town's newspaper, the Eldorado *Republican*, was in the second year of his term as a state senator. Murdock, who had been elected with the support of the Santa Fe Railroad, was one cog in the political machine that ran the state. To edit the *Republican* during his own frequent absences in the state capital, he hired a rather brash young man called William Allen White. In January 1890, when he took over the paper, White was a self-confessed child of the ruling class, with a taste in clothes that ran to long Prince Albert coats and pongee silk shirts. The gaudy attire was somewhat misleading, for if the new editor was extravagant in dress, he was deeply conservative in most other things. Not yet twenty-two, White already saw himself as a defender of the existing political order. The trouble was that in Kansas, by 1890, that existing order was under attack.

Across the state, the farmers were girding themselves

Freedom, peace, and harmony with nature are the qualities of rural life emphasized in John Steuart Curry's paintings. But depression and debt were equally familiar to farmers after the Civil War.

for battle. Of all groups in society, they had been the most badly affected when drought hit Kansas in 1887, wiping out the great economic boom of the 1870s and 1880s. Most farmers had borrowed heavily during the boom years to make improvements to their farms. With the collapse, they found themselves seriously overextended. Many sold out and left the state, trekking back eastward in wagons painted with such bitter legends as "In God we trusted, in Kansas we busted." Those who remained continued to suffer under a heavy burden of debt. In 1890, in some of the counties of central Kansas around Eldorado, three-quarters of all farms were mortgaged. Simultaneously confronted with falling prices for their crops and high interest payments, at a time when money was in short supply, the farmers began to press for political action to help them out of their difficulties. Many of their complaints centered on exploitation by railroads, warehouses, and mortgage companies. But when they appealed to the state government for assistance, they found it more sympathetic to the exploiters than to the exploited.

To beat politicians like Murdock and through them the railroads, the farmers were compelled to enter politics themselves. Since neither of the two major parties was sympathetic to their cause, they were obliged to act through organizations of their own: first the Farmers' Alliance, and then the new Populist party.

The Farmers' Alliance was the broad organizational term for the two major agrarian reform groups which followed from the decline of their predecessor, the Granger

movement. The Northern Alliance comprised the farming states from Ohio to the Dakotas; and the Southern Alliance included Louisiana, Arkansas, and Texas. As well as the sectional groups, each of the member states organized themselves into local or state-wide alliances. In the summer of 1890, the Kansas Alliance put up a state ticket of its own for the fall elections. Supporters of the Republican and Democratic parties scoffed at the farmers' candidates as "the riffraff, rag, tag, and bobtail" of Kansas society— farmers without farms, storekeepers without stores, and lawyers without practices. But the regular parties underestimated the importance of agrarian distress. During the summer of 1890, townsfolk riding out at night began to notice little country schoolhouses that were all lit up once or twice a week for political meetings. Before the other parties had even held their conventions, the farmers were off and running. It would be only two years before the Populists captured the governorship of Kansas, and "Sockless" Jerry Simpson stood on the steps of the Statehouse to declare that the seat of government had been removed "from the Santa Fe offices, back to the Statehouse where it belongs."

Kansas was in many ways a microcosm of what was happening elsewhere in the United States. Throughout the West and the South—wherever farmers were troubled by falling prices for their produce and crushed beneath a weight of unpaid mortgages—the same stirrings were taking place. It was the sudden strength of the farmers' revolt that took contemporaries by surprise. In the spring of 1890, William Allen White dismissed the Farmers' Alliance as "just another of those farmer cooperatives which would start a store and maybe build an elevator, last two or three years, and then dry up and blow away." White was wrong, as it happened, but his assessment seemed reasonable at the time. There was little reason to suppose that the Farmers' Alliance would be any different from earlier movements of agrarian protest.

The first major cooperative movement of American postwar farmers began before memory of the flush times accompanying wartime inflation had altogether faded. In 1867 Oliver Hudson Kelley founded a secret society to be called the Patrons of Husbandry. Kelley, a clerk in the United States Bureau of Agriculture, had cut his teeth on farmers' troubles during his boyhood in Minnesota. In 1866 he traveled through the states of the old Confederacy as a field investigator for his bureau. Everywhere he went, even in the war-torn South, Kelley was less impressed with economic damage than he was with the spiritual and cultural poverty present in rural areas. He set out to do something about it. The Patrons of Husbandry, more popularly known as the Grange (from the archaic term they used to describe their local meeting-place), had a program that was largely social and educational. It shrewdly appealed to women as well as to men: farmers were encouraged to enroll their wives and daughters,

who then became eligible to hold office in the society alongside their menfolk.

The Grange got off to a slow start, since farmers were reluctant to organize at a time when they seemed to be doing well on their own. Minnesota, where much of the early effort was concentrated, had only thirty-seven Granges by the end of 1869. It took the pinch of hard times, which began in the early 1870s, to get the Granger movement off the ground. Once driven to desperation, the farmers were prepared to join anything that seemed to hold out reasonable promise for their relief. This was to be the pattern of agrarian movements from the 1860s to the 1890s. During good times, the independent farmer tended to see himself as a hardheaded business entrepreneur. He stood self-confidently on his own feet, spurning membership in organizations devoted to the betterment of his condition. When lean years came to threaten his independence and his livelihood, he retreated into the guise of the misunderstood yeoman farmer, preyed on by the alien forces of capital and industry. While in this frame of mind, he was ready to band together with his comrades in misfortune. But once the immediate crisis passed, his interest in collective action began to wane.

In the early 1870s membership of the Grange soared. The panic year of 1873 alone saw the birth of more than 8,000 new granges. As the organization expanded in scope, its priorities changed. Plans for social and educational betterment now took second place to the attack on more pressing problems. The farmers were particularly troubled by the cost of transporting their produce. In the West, where the railroads faced no competition from canals or waterways, their implied motto was all too often "Charge all the traffic will bear." Freight rates west of the Missouri could be as much as four times as high as those east of the river. It took one bushel of grain, protested western farmers, to pay the cost of freight for a second bushel. Especially in those states north and west of Chicago that suffered most from the problem, the Grangers came together to demand state regulation of the rates charged by railroads and elevator companies. Another major grievance was the gap between what the farmer paid his local dealer for manufactured goods, and the actual cost of their production. In 1874, the National Grange suggested "working together, buying together, selling together, and generally acting together for . . . mutual protection and advancement." Cooperation among farmers would cut costs by eliminating unnecessary middlemen.

The theory was a nice one, but in practice neither rate regulation nor cooperative action proved as successful as the farmers had hoped. The railroads fought state regulation all the way up to the United States Supreme Court, which in 1876 ruled in favor of the legality of the "Granger" laws. By then, it was too late. The railroads

Only by united action could farm families in the Midwest hope to reap harvests as bounteous as this picture suggests. The Grange movement sought to protect the farmers during the lean years.

had already undercut the effectiveness of regulation. In Illinois after 1871 they simply refused to abide by the maximum freight and passenger rates fixed by the legislature. Travelers who insisted on paying only the legal fare were summarily ejected. In Wisconsin the railroads threw a *cordon sanitaire* around the state, cutting their service to the unfortunate farmers until the legislature surrendered and repealed its offensive rate law. By the end of the 1870s most of the "Granger" laws had either been repealed or rendered ineffective.

The farmers, it seemed, could achieve temporary unity at a time of maximum distress, but were unequal to the task of sustaining their hard-won victories in a long, drawn-out campaign. Membership of the Grange began to fall as early as 1875 and by the end of the decade it had ceased to exist as a political force. Much the same story of early success and swift decline could be told of the Grange's efforts at cooperation. The farmers set off in high spirits to manufacture their own harvesters. They established their own retail cooperatives, grain elevators, and creameries. They sold a little insurance and experimented with meat-packing and the milling of grain. But such widely diffused energies soon began to flag. The Grangers had little hard experience in methods of cooperation. They remained perennially suspicious of others and were too easily discouraged by faltering progress. They benefited when Montgomery Ward and Company introduced mail-order purchase in 1872, but most of their own cooperative efforts quickly faded. Facing a decline in both numbers and enthusiasm, local granges went back to their original aim of improving rural life.

The next major agrarian movement was the Farmers' Alliance, which was to suffer similar fluctuations in membership. The first effective alliance organization in the North was founded in Cook County, Illinois, in 1880. Its moving spirit was Milton George, sometime farmer and now editor of the *Western Rural*, a Chicago farm journal. George publicized the alliance idea in the pages of his magazine, but the best recruiting agent was still hard times.

At the end of the 1870s midwestern farmers produced bumper crops that tended to push prices down. During 1879 and 1880, increasing exports to Europe absorbed much of the surplus, but the situation changed in 1881 when drought hit the upper Mississippi Valley. The alliance came to enjoy a brief vogue in those states like Kansas, Nebraska, Iowa, and Minnesota where the drought hit hardest. Then, in the period immediately after 1883, good crops and fair prices took the edge off the demand for alliance-style protest. Interest revived once more

The Grange movement got off to a slow start in 1867 and reached its peak in the 1870s. This poster, which appeared in 1873, reminded members of the virtues of hard work and frugality.

during the fall and winter of 1884–85, when wheat prices fell; and for once this proved no mere flash in the pan. Instead of the usual pattern of swift expansion followed by a rapid decline, it began to seem to men like Milton George that the farmers of the Middle Border were at last becoming class-conscious. Over the next few years, the Farmers' Alliance increased its membership enormously. By 1890, new members were flocking to join at the rate of over a thousand a week. The Kansas alliance alone claimed 130,000 supporters, and branches in neighboring states where times were almost equally hard did not lag very far behind. "The people," exulted the editor of the *Western Rural,* "are aroused at last."

In the meantime, a similar but distinct alliance movement was under way in the South. Beginning in Texas, the order claimed a membership of 50,000 in that state by December 1885. Nominally apolitical, the Texas alliance all but ruined itself when it made the mistake of becoming involved in the state elections of 1886. The articulate C. W. Macune rescued it from disaster. Born in Wisconsin in 1851, Macune inherited a roving temperament from his father. Before settling in Texas, he had already lived in Illinois, Kansas, and California. He was nothing if not versatile. At the age of ten, he quit school to work on a farm. Later, he practiced medicine and also dabbled in law. An able speaker and a fluent writer, he became chairman of the executive committee of the Texas alliance in 1886. His first idea was to expand the organization in order to distract the attention of Texas alliance men from squabbles at home. For a while, he toyed with the idea of amalgamation with the Northern Alliance. When the practical difficulties in the way of this seemed for the moment insuperable, he turned to the alternative scheme of organizing the southern cotton growers. The moment was opportune. Plagued by low prices, the depredations of country merchants, and the unfortunate crop-lien system, these farmers were desperate for relief. Macune shrewdly presented the alliance to them as a hardheaded, businesslike organization, offering "the substance of things hoped for, the evidence of things not seen. . . ." Hoping that the alliance would help get them out of debt and on the way to eventual profit, the cotton farmers rushed to join. By 1890 the Southern Alliance had a membership of between 1 million and 3 million.

Differences between the Northern and Southern Alliances continued to impede the efforts of unification, even when both alliances held simultaneous meetings at St Louis in 1889. Southerners objected to the loose organization of the Northern Alliance, its nonsecret nature, and the fact that it admitted Negroes. Sectional prejudices continued. One hostile Kansas editor branded the entire alliance movement in the South as a "rebel yell." Both alliances took pride in their educational efforts, their program of social events, and their occasional forays into the world of business. But they were beginning to realize that what the farmer really needed was political action to secure favorable legislation from Congress. The idea of a third-party movement had already been seriously mooted in the North, but southern farmers still seemed wedded to the Democratic party. Union of the two alliances in such circumstances might have proved embarrassing to those northerners who were pushing for independent action. Although the St Louis conference of 1889 failed to agree on amalgamation, it had shown both northern and southern farmers to be in substantial agreement on their aims; this was significant. Should a new party appear, it would find its platform ready and waiting.

The turning point for the idea of a third party came with the elections of 1890. Alliance conventions in Kansas and other midwestern states drew up their own local and state tickets. In the South, disgruntled farmers set out to take over the regular Democratic party machinery. The election results, when they came, were startling enough. In Kansas, William Allen White watched with unconcealed wonder as the alliance missed capturing the governorship by a whisker, and went on to win control of the state house of representatives. Throughout Nebraska, Minnesota, and South Dakota, alliance candidates showed surprising strength. In the South, the old Democratic guard was humiliated in South Carolina, Georgia, and Tennessee. Elsewhere it suffered a mighty scare. More conscious now of their strength, the alliances began to give more and more serious consideration to the movement for a third party. And in the months after the election, as southern farmers discovered that their local successes cut little ice with the Democratic politicians in Washington, the last major obstacle in the way of such a movement began to disappear.

The Birth of the Populists

Three years before, St Louis had been the scene of unsuccessful attempts at union between the Northern and Southern Alliances. On February 22, 1892, the city again began to fill with "gray-haired, sunburned and roughly clothed men. . . ." With an almost religious fervor, the newcomers came to draw up the program of a new party. Noisy and determined, they sat beneath a large poster bearing the unequivocal words: "We do not ask for sympathy. We ask for justice." When the platform of the newly born People's (or Populist) party emerged, it was accompanied by a preamble that formed a stunning indictment of American society. Read to the convention by its author, Ignatius Donnelly of Minnesota, it sounded less like a political tract than some vision of the apocalypse. "We meet," cried Donnelly, "in the midst of a nation brought to the verge of moral, political and material ruin. Corruption dominates the ballot box, the legislatures,

the Congress, and touches even the ermine of the bench. The people are demoralized. . . . The newspapers are subsidized or muzzled; public opinion silenced; business prostrated, our homes covered with mortgages, labor impoverished, and the land concentrating in the hands of capitalists." Once Donnelly had finished, Hugh Kavanaugh, chairman of the platform committee, stepped forward to read the actual demands. As he in turn concluded, the convention erupted in a shouting, cheering demonstration that lasted without interruption for ten minutes, and reminded one observer of "the lashing of the ocean against a rocky beach during a hurricane. . . ."

There was little that was new in the St Louis platform. For the most part, it represented a drawing together of demands made by the farmers in the past. It called for an increase in the amount of money in circulation and demanded the free and unlimited coinage of silver. It asked for a graduated income tax and the establishment of postal savings banks. It attacked land speculation and monopolistic ownership. It endorsed the subtreasury scheme that aimed to enable farmers to raise low-interest loans from the federal government on the strength of their depositing nonperishable agricultural goods in government elevators and warehouses. Finally, and here they flirted closely with socialism, the farmers called for the public ownership of the railroads and of telephone and telegraph services.

The impact of the Populist program can be gauged from the changing attitude of the public toward the railroads. Many farmers traveled to the St Louis convention with the assistance of railroad-fare concessions. Four-and-a half months later, when the Populists met in Omaha to nominate a national candidate, the railroads refused them all concessions. Far from dismayed, the delegates roared their approval as Marion Cannon of California shouted back, "We can stand the refusal!"

Populism drew most of its political strength from three main areas of the United States. At its most radical, in the South, it was a movement against the "Bourbon" leaders of the Democratic party. Since Reconstruction days, these men had preserved their power by playing on the antipathy of poor whites toward poor blacks. To the Populists, who saw the South's main problem as one of poverty and not race, this seemed tragically wrong. They became the first American political party to attempt the formation of a coalition between the disadvantaged of both races. In the West, Populism was primarily a movement against corporate power, particularly the railroads. In Nebraska, to the tune of "Save a Poor Sinner like Me," the farmers were accustomed to sing how "the railroads and old party bosses did sweetly agree" to rob and deceive "a hayseed like me." Western Populists sought to disrupt the cozy alliance that had grown up between business and politics. Both the South and the West, heavily dependent on the export market, were regions

A patched-up balloon of hot air and failed splinter groups is how this cartoonist saw the People's party in 1891. But the next year the party surprised its critics by polling over a million votes in the presidential election.

of one-crop farming. They suffered disproportionately from problems of transportation and mortgage-indebtedness. The third area of Populist strength was markedly different in both character and preoccupation. For in the Rocky Mountain states of Colorado, Wyoming, and Montana, the great issue centered not so much on farming as on free silver; the metal was mined in those states.

It Must Be a Conspiracy!

In April 1895, at the height of the Populist revolt, a Mississippi congressman wrote Cleveland's secretary of war that ''A little free silver book called 'Coin's Financial School' is being sold on every railroad train by the newsboys and at every cigar store. . . . It is being read by everybody.'' William Hope Harvey, the author of that

little book, had been by turn schoolteacher, lawyer, real estate agent, and promoter of a curious quack potion he called his ''Elixir of Life.'' Sometime during the 1880s, he spent three years superintending the working of a silver mine in Colorado. The mine was a productive one, although the price of silver itself, which had declined disastrously during the 1870s, continued to fall. Harvey became disillusioned with mining, but by May 1893 had made enough out of his real estate business to move to Chicago. There he set up a publishing house dedicated to the advocacy of free silver. In 1894 he published *Coin's Financial School*, a 155-page treatise written in the form of six ''lectures.'' Harvey brought to the currency issue a mind unencumbered by any practical knowledge of economics. He wrote from the bitter school of his own experience in silver mining. But his arrival in Chicago coincided with the beginning of the great depression of the 1890s; the economic distress helped give his writings a certain specious appeal.

Harvey drew on the frustration felt by the American farmer at deflation and falling prices. He offered an arresting "conspiracy" theory to explain the demonetization of silver as a plot on the part of British bankers and Jewish moneylenders. Silver, the "poor man's friend," was associated with prosperity and inflation. When the Coinage Act of 1873 omitted to recognize the silver dollar, the omission was all part of a scheme on the part of international bondholders to obtain payment in gold. Free-silverites pointed darkly to the financial panic that occurred just seven months after this "Crime of '73." The price of silver began to fall at around the same time; so too did the prices of wheat and cotton. And while strict chronology might have undermined the assumption that the demonetization of silver began the great deflation of the 1870s, the free-silverites were not interested in strict chronology. They were propagandists of a faith. Indeed, the remarkable thing about the free-silver agitation was its exemplary devotion to a creed that had little relation to cold fact.

The inflation during the Civil War, which the farmers looked back upon with nostalgia, had nothing to do with silver. In 1861 the United States government suspended payments of its currency in specie and instead issued Treasury notes, the famous "greenbacks," as full legal tender. In effect, the nation was now on an inconvertible paper standard. Greenbacks could not normally be exchanged for either gold or silver specie.

In the years after Appomattox, advocates of "sound money" began to push for the retirement of the greenbacks and a restoration of specie payments. This was resisted by some western businessmen and by most farmers, who feared the deflationary consequences of any contraction in available currency. The first inflationist movement after the Civil War was pro-greenback rather than pro-silver, and a Greenback party had some success at the polls in the late 1870s. All to no avail. The "sound money" men were in charge of national policy. In 1875 Congress passed the Specie Resumption Act which provided for a return to specie payments on January 1, 1879. Since the Coinage Act of 1873 had "demonetized" silver, it was obvious that such specie payments would necessarily be in gold.

The problem with the "Crime of '73" was that, far from being the result of a surreptitious plot, it was merely the recognition of existing reality. As the inflationists switched their allegiance from greenbacks to silver, they made the assumption that silver had been in circulation before 1873. Despite, or perhaps because of, the nominally bimetallic standard—that is, gold and silver—that had prevailed since the 1790s, this inflationist view was far from being the case. A bimetallic currency, all right in theory, tends in practice to result in one precious metal becoming dominant. Before 1834, the United States was effectively on a silver standard. After 1834, when Congress changed the mint ratio between gold and silver, gold came to predominate. The emotion of the free-silverites for "the dollar of our daddies" becomes rather spurious when we remember that Jefferson stopped the coining of silver dollars as early as 1806. Even before 1834, there were few in circulation, and by 1873 they were almost forgotten. The Coinage Act made no mention of the silver dollar because, in practical terms, silver had already been demonetized.

The Populists inherited much of the folklore of free silver. It was easier to believe that falling prices were the result of an international "gold-bug" conspiracy than to see the root cause in American overproduction. This was as true of cotton and wheat as it was of silver. Something in the plight of the American farmer made him susceptible to paranoia. Brooding in the isolation of his farm, he felt victimized by northeastern industry, secure behind its protective wall of tariffs. The farmer sold his crop on the world market, where competition helped keep prices low; he bought his goods in a protected market designed to keep prices up. The farmer felt aggrieved; unlike the businessman, he invested not only his own labor and capital in his work but also the labor of his family. If he lost his farm, he lost his home.

As his economic troubles multiplied, the farmer became increasingly conscious of his declining social status. Accustomed since Jeffersonian days to see himself, however inaccurately, as an independent yeoman figure, he was now beset by doubt. It was more and more evident that sophisticated city-dwellers looked down upon him as a "hayseed," a rustic figure of fun. The farmer fed the city only to be rewarded with contempt. Worse, it housed many of his tormentors, from elevators and railroad offices to banks and mortgage companies.

All of this encouraged the farmer to see the city as a parasite—living, as it did, off the countryside. He was convinced of his own importance, for without the food he provided no city could survive. William Jennings Bryan caught this feeling in his "Cross of Gold" speech of 1896, when he argued that "The great cities rest upon our broad and fertile prairies. . . ." Yet however much the farmer railed against what he considered the sinful, immigrant-infested city, his children were often eager to live there. To them, it represented opportunity, the chance for a fuller life after the rigors of years spent on the farm. Baffled and confused at such a repudiation of his own values, the farmer talked of exploitive "money trusts," spawned by Jewish bankers and English gold. He denounced the East with its bankers and businessmen, the city with its temptations and tenements.

William Jennings Bryan's ringing declaration, "You shall not crucify mankind upon a cross of gold," caused public outrage. Bryan was accused of blasphemy for mixing Biblical imagery with political ideology.

COPYRIGHT 1896, BY THE JUDGE PUBLISHING COMPANY OF NEW YORK.

The Spectrum of Populist Leadership

If the ideology of Populism was colorful, so too were its leaders. From Georgia came cantankerous Tom Watson, thirty-six years old in 1892. Born on a southern farm, Watson had scratched his way upwards to become a highly competent criminal lawyer. But the climb itself told on his character: he was perennially suspicious of the motives of others, a difficult man and one cursed with a flaming temper. Tom Watson was low-tariff and pro-Cleveland in 1888. Thereafter, he came to believe that the tariff was less important politically than the money question. He became a natural leader of the Farmers' Alliance, was elected to Congress in 1890, and later gave his support to the Populist program.

"Pitchfork Ben" Tillman, the "one-eyed plowboy" from South Carolina, was even more intemperate and vituperative than Watson. Born in the back country of his state, close to the Georgia border, Tillman came from a family that was neither rich nor poor. His father, who died young, kept an inn and owned both land and slaves. His remarkable mother worked long and hard to improve the position of the family. After the Civil War, she gave young Benjamin a 400-acre farm on which to live. Everything went well for Tillman until 1881, when, he said, "the devil tempted me to buy a steam engine and other machinery, amounting to two thousand dollars, all on credit." Drought and crop failure added to the difficulties of repayment and finally forced the sale of much of his land. Tillman was a bitter man and a deadly one: three of his brothers died violent deaths, another committed homicide in a drunken brawl. But in 1890 "Pitchfork Ben," for all his faults, was elected governor of South Carolina.

The Omaha convention picked General James B. Weaver to be the Populist standard-bearer in the election of 1892. A seasoned campaigner, with a reputation more safe than spectacular, Weaver had first run for the White House in 1880 on the Greenbacker ticket. The West produced other third-party veterans, congenital crusaders like Ignatius Donnelly of Minnesota. The plumpish Donnelly, with his friendly smile and Irish eloquence, had broken a lance for almost every movement of political dissent since antislavery. To hold a convention of Minnesota reformers without him, quipped the New York *Sun*, would be "like catfish without waffles in Philadelphia."

Kansas produced more than its share of Populist agitators. Mrs Mary Lease, who brought up four children before being admitted to the bar in 1885, made over 160 speeches for the alliance during the heated campaign of 1890. In 1892 she toured the state again, preaching Populism and advising the farmers to raise "less corn and

more hell." Just as dedicated as Mrs Lease was Senator William A. Peffer, editor of the *Kansas Farmer*, a man who seemed to one observer like "something Hebraic—something intense, narrow, and fanatical." From Kansas, too, came Jerry Simpson, the only man ever to become nationally famous on the basis of a totally false accusation that he never wore socks. Like Donnelly, Simpson was well known in third-party circles. From their own experience, both men recognized that to be successful Populism must appeal beyond the farm. Donnelly put his faith in an alliance between farmers and the workingmen of the cities. Simpson urged an appeal based on the ideas of Henry George.

Three Radical Voices

One day in January 1865, a well-dressed man walking down a San Francisco street was approached by a stranger who asked him for five dollars. He needed the money, explained Henry George, because his wife was about to give birth to their second child and he had no money for food. Eight years earlier, George had left home in Philadelphia with the bright hope of becoming, as his mother had put it, "something and somebody in the world." But whether as storekeeper, printer, or partner in an ill-fated San Francisco newspaper, misfortune seemed to dog his footsteps. When he proposed to Annie Fox in 1861, he took a 50-cent piece out of his pocket and said, "Annie, this is all the money I have in the world. Will you marry me?" Four more years of unrelenting struggle to make a living, and George made this grim note in his diary: "I have been unsuccessful in everything."

Yet he continued to dream of what he called "the Golden Age . . . when the poorest and meanest will have a chance to use all his God-given faculties, and not be forced to drudge away the best part of his time to support wants but little above those of the animal." Like other Californians, Henry George could not understand a situation in which poverty proliferated as fast as wealth. He knew that much land in his state was owned by eastern capitalists and absentee landlords who drew large unearned incomes from their property. But only in 1870 did it finally become clear to him that while population growth increases the value of land, it also increases the cost of the rent for using that land.

If George was right, poverty and unemployment were the result of one class's power to preempt society's increased wealth through rent. Land monopoly was the basic source of inequality in American society. Henry George had identified his enemy; he had not yet determined how best to attack it. But during the 1870s his conviction grew that there could be "no work so great as a great book." In 1877 he set out to write that book,

Right and center: Brown Brothers

Library of Congress

Left to right: Henry George, Edward Bellamy, and Henry Demarest Lloyd. Forum *magazine called this trio of articulate reformers the "Prophets of Unrest." George introduced the idea of the single tax to reduce the gulf between rich and poor. Bellamy proposed a more even distribution of wealth as poverty's cure. The panacea for Lloyd was an end to the monopolistic practices employed by big business, in particular those carried out by Standard Oil.*

laboring on for nearly two years at his self-imposed task. Finally, in the middle of a March night in 1879, the last sentence of *Progress and Poverty* was written. Overcome by emotion, George knelt on the floor weeping: as a man he had done all he could—the rest "lay in the Master's hands."

His book argued that poverty would only be abolished when land monopoly itself was abolished. It looked forward to the day when land would be the common property of all. In the meantime, it advocated heavy taxation on land values, the prelude to the idea of a "single tax" on land. By the end of the 1880s, there would be a full-fledged, single tax movement looking to George for leadership. But for the moment what mattered was that as the sales of *Progress and Poverty*, slow at first, began to build up on both sides of the Atlantic, Henry George had at last achieved his mother's wish that he become "somebody."

In 1890, E. R. A. Seligman of Columbia University debated George in public. The professor thought Georgian economics far too simple, and was particularly critical of the emphasis placed by the single-taxers on land monopoly. He argued that Edward Bellamy's "nationalist" movement had grown at George's expense because it recognized other sources of unearned profit beside land. Few men could ever have been less plausible as the leader of a political movement than the shy, retiring

Bellamy, who in 1888 described his occupation as "journalist and fiction writer." But, born at Chicopee Falls, Massachusetts, in 1850, Bellamy was a Yankee to the core, deeply imbued with what one historian has called "the Brook Farm temperament." An incorrigible optimist with a deep faith in the millennium, he was saddened by the rampant commercialism and industrial violence that characterized American society in the 1880s. In 1886, the year of the Haymarket bomb outrage in Chicago, he began work on a book that recommended fundamental social changes, dressed up and served in the guise of utopian fiction.

Looking Backward, published in 1888, told the story of Julian West, hero extraordinary, who is mesmerized into a deep sleep in 1887 and wakes up in the year 2000. Guided by his genial host, Dr Leete, West is introduced to a society which has eliminated the brutality and waste of cutthroat competition. It possesses untold wealth, for as Dr Leete phrases it, "Competition, which is the instinct of selfishness, is another word for dissipation of energy, while combination is the secret of efficient production." All wealth is social wealth: private enterprise has been abolished, or rather "nationalised." What Bellamy was really offering to Americans was socialism by the back door, under a new name. But he was shrewd enough to excite the imagination of middle-class intellectuals and professional men with his vision of a new society. By 1890, *Looking Backward* had sold nearly a quarter of a million copies, and "nationalist" clubs devoted to Bellamy's ideas had sprung up all over the United States.

In August 1890, an article in the *Forum* magazine bracketed Bellamy and George with Henry Demarest Lloyd as the three "Prophets of Unrest." Bellamy attacked cutthroat competition in industry for its wastefulness; Lloyd concerned himself with the ethics of such competition and also the monopolistic tendencies it encouraged. Born in New York in 1849, the son of a pastor in the Dutch Reformed Church, Lloyd grew up with a strongly moralistic attitude toward the world. He and his brothers were encouraged by their mother to "acquire some practice" for the "fight . . . with evil and wickedness" in "this crooked world." Young Henry's early career was very much that of the New York patrician: Columbia College, Class of '67; law school; a spell of working for the Free Trade League. In 1872, Horace White lured him away from New York with the offer of the night city-editorship of the Chicago *Tribune.* But unlike most men, who tend to become more conservative as they grow older, Henry Demarest Lloyd became more open-minded and radical. As a Chicago journalist, he began to write attacks on railroads and monopolies.

In the years that followed, Lloyd became more and more convinced that unrestrained capitalism was immoral in operation and socially destructive in its results. In 1889, he decided to write a book that would chronicle the rise of monopoly in business, using John D. Rockefeller's Standard Oil Company as the prototype of a monopolistic organization. The research for that book took him five-and-a-half years, and revealed a story of "human greed and cruelty almost too nauseous to handle." *Wealth Against Commonwealth,* published in

1894, depicted Rockefeller as a "Czar of plutocracy," building up his South Improvement Company into the mammoth Standard Oil by means of railroad rebates, conspiracy, bribery, and industrial espionage. Although it sold far fewer copies than either *Progress and Poverty* or *Looking Backward, Wealth Against Commonwealth* was a powerful indictment of the gigantic fortunes built up by a few men using methods that were unethical if not downright illegal. It helped impress on many educated minds Lloyd's concern that "Liberty and monopoly cannot live together . . . political brotherhood cannot survive where industrial brotherhood is denied."

Revolt and Depression

Both capital and labor became more militant during the 1890s, and neither showed very much evidence of "industrial brotherhood." Employers responded to strikes with court injunctions, "scab" labor, lockouts, "yellow-dog"

On President Cleveland's orders an army regiment was sent to Chicago in July 1894 to suppress the Pullman strikers. An eyewitness sketched this scene Giving the Butt *to portray army tactics.*

Three Lions

contracts, and private armies of detectives. During the summer of 1892, a strike in the Carnegie Steel Works at Homestead, Pennsylvania, resulted in a pitched battle between strikers and about 300 Pinkerton agents (industrial police) sent to guard the plant and protect "scab" labor. Two years later, those who knew of the "model town" George M. Pullman had built for his workers outside Chicago were surprised to hear that industrial trouble had flared up there. But Pullman's philanthropy was far from selfless, and economist Richard T. Ely found the very idea of such a "benevolent, well-wishing feudalism" fundamentally "un-American." A Pullman worker put the matter succinctly when he said: "We are born in a Pullman house, fed from a Pullman shop, taught in the Pullman school, catechized in the Pullman church, and when we die we shall be buried in a Pullman cemetery." In 1894, although Pullman reduced the wages of his workers, rents in his model village were kept at the same level. The result was a strike that soon threatened to paralyze all American railroads. Pullman cars were burned and strike-breakers assaulted; a federal court issued a "blanket" injunction to restrain the strikers. Eugene V. Debs, president of the American Railway Union, was arrested and imprisoned. Finally, without a shred of constitutional authority and over the vigorous protest of

Governor Altgeld of Illinois, President Cleveland effectively ended the strike by dispatching federal troops to Chicago.

In the summer of 1893, a financial panic brought industrial depression in its wake and worsened the agricultural depression that already existed. Unemployment rose as production fell: 2.5 million workers were out of work during the winter of 1893–94. Such mass misery produced colorful forms of protest, particularly the march of various industrial "armies" of unemployed to Washington, in the pathetic hope of obtaining relief. The most famous of these armies was "General" Jacob S. Coxey's "Commonweal of Christ," which set off from Massillon, Ohio, in March 1894. A young Chicago journalist, Ray Stannard Baker, tramped with the army as it moved slowly towards Washington along roads that were frequently quagmires, and over mountains sometimes a foot deep in snow. Initially he was half-amused at the grotesqueness of Coxey's protest, but finally Baker came to see it as a genuine "manifestation of the prevailing unrest and dissatisfaction among the laboring classes."

Few thought that Jacob Coxey and his band of 100 unemployed men would complete their march from Ohio to the nation's capital. This photograph shows the "army," now 500 strong, on the outskirts of Washington.

The march itself ended in fiasco, when Coxey and his deputy, the preposterous Carl Browne, were arrested for walking on the grass around the Capitol. Nonetheless Coxeyism demonstrated more dramatically than anything else the seriousness of the economic crisis that faced the nation.

The End of the Populist Saga

It was unfortunate for Grover Cleveland that the second term of his presidency should have coincided with the depression of 1893–97. Cleveland was a bluff liberal of the old, classical school; in 1888 he vetoed a bill to help farmers suffering from drought on the grounds that "though the people support the government the government should not support the people."

Cleveland regarded the depression as the product of business operations. Its cure was up to business alone. The most that the federal government could be expected to do was to maintain a sound and stable currency. In practice, as Cleveland interpreted it, this meant a rigid adherence to the gold standard. In 1893 he called a special session of Congress to repeal the Sherman Silver Purchase Act of 1890, which obliged the secretary of the Treasury to buy a modest 4.5 million ounces of silver each month. To secure repeal, the president was obliged to ride roughshod over the many Democratic supporters of silver. By the time he signed the bill into law on November 1, 1893, the unity of his party was shattered.

In an attempt to restore Democratic unity, Cleveland revived his 1887 demand for a downward revision of the tariff. But the Democrats now proved themselves no more united on the tariff than upon anything else. The protectionist Wilson-Gorman Tariff Act that finally emerged was far from being a true reform; in fact most of the changes were upward. Taken together, the events of 1893–94 seem to have convinced Americans that Cleveland's administration was incapable of dealing with the economic crisis. In the fall elections of 1894, the Republicans won control of both houses of Congress. In twenty-four states, not a single Democrat was elected to a federal office.

When the Populist convention met at St Louis in the summer of 1896, it also nominated Bryan. As a half-hearted attempt to preserve its own identity, the party chose Tom Watson as its vice-presidential candidate, instead of Arthur Sewall of Maine, the Democratic nominee. The campaign that followed was the most exciting and

Coxey had hoped to solicit federal relief for the unemployed, but was prevented by police from reading his demands to the May Day crowd at the Capitol. This photograph was taken after he was apprehended.

divisive in a generation. Gold and silver were not just precious metals: they became veritable symbols of faith. William McKinley of Ohio, the Republican nominee, ran with the support of business as a "sound money" man dedicated to the preservation of the gold standard. Bryan, whose natural constituency was the underprivileged, offered them a remedy for their distress based on tinkering with the monetary system.

By October, Bryan's one-issue campaign was running out of steam. Free silver had been strong enough to wrest control of the Democratic party away from Cleveland and the "gold-bugs": it was not enough, however, to win a national election. Silver inflation might have helped the farmer solve some of his problems, but rising prices were the last thing urban labor wanted at a time of low wages and weak unions. Bryan carried the areas of Populist strength in the West and the South, but failed to dent McKinley's margin in the industrial Northeast. Nothing illustrated the weakness of Bryan's appeal to labor more than the deputation of Homestead workers who called on McKinley to offer him their support. Four years after the bloody confrontation at the Carnegie works, it was the candidate of the Republican party, predicting fifty-three-cent dollars if his opponent was elected, who emerged as the "advance guard" of prosperity.

There were many who felt with Henry Demarest Lloyd that free silver, "the cowbird of the reform movement," had caused a great opportunity to be missed. The defeat of 1896 all but finished Populism as an independent force. Many western Populists formally joined the Democratic party. In the South, the regular Democrats recaptured power by reviving the old Reconstruction bogey of "nigger domination" to separate the poor of both races. As the increased international supply of gold at the end of the century caused prices at last to rise, the long agrarian depression came to an end. Then came the Spanish-American War, which drowned cries for reform in what Tom Watson dourly called "the blare of the bugle."

Populism was essentially a revolt on the part of producers who felt themselves excluded from the benefits of a rapidly urbanizing, increasingly industrial society. But even in 1896, Bryan lost states like Illinois and Wisconsin where, already, farmers had come to terms with the new America. The rise of large urban markets encouraged dairying and the more stable "corn and hog complex" type of farming. It lessened the farmer's dependence on a single cash crop grown for export. And in the years after 1897, as the figure of the shaggy agrarian reformer disappeared, his attack on corruption and privilege was taken up by others. Populism was the first political movement to attack head-on the evils of industrialism. In so doing, it prepared the way for the attempt to humanize society through law that lay close to the heart of middle-class progressivism.

Bibliography

GENERAL

Brock, William R., *Investigation and Responsibility: Public Responsibility in the United States, 1865-1900* (New York, 1984)

Degler, Carl N., *The Age of the Economic Revolution, 1876-1900* (Glenview, III., 1967)

Ginger, Ray, *Age of Excess: The United States from 1877 to 1914* (New York, 1965)

Hays, Samuel P., *The Response to Industrialism, 1885-1914* (Chicago, 1957)

Keller, Morton, *Affairs of State: Public Life in Late Nineteenth-Century America* (Cambridge, Mass., 1977)

Morgan, H. Wayne, ed., *The Gilded Age: A Reappraisal* (Syracuse, 1963)

Morgan, H. Wayne, *Unity and Culture: The United States, 1877-1900* (Baltimore, 1971)

Nevins, Allan, *The Emergence of Modern America, 1865-1878* (New York, 1927)

Shannon, Fred A., *The Centennial Years: A Political and Economic History of America from the late 1870's to the early 1890's* (Garden City, N.Y., 1967)

Tarbell, Ida M., *The Nationalizing of Business, 1878-1898* (New York, 1936)

Walker, Robert H., *Life in the Age of Enterprise, 1865-1900* (New York, 1971)

Weisberger, Bernard A., *The New Industrial Society, 1848-1900* (New York, 1969)

Wiebe, Robert H. *The Search for Order, 1877-1920* (New York, 1967)

Chapter 1: AN INDUSTRIAL NATION

The Triumph of Big Business

Andreano, Ralph, ed., *The Economic Impact of the American Civil War* (Cambridge, Mass., 1967)

Clark, Victor S., *History of Manufactures in the United States, 1860-1914* (Washington, D.C., 1929)

Cochran, Thomas C., *Railroad Leaders, 1845-1890* (Cambridge, Mass., 1953)

Cochran, Thomas C., & Miller, William, *The Age of Enterprise* (New York, 1942)

Fine, Sidney, *Laissez Faire and the General Welfare State, 1865-1901* (Ann Arbor, Mich., 1956)

Hawke, David F., *John D: The Founding Father of the Rockefellers* (New York, 1980)

Josephson, Matthew, *The Robber Barons: The Great American Capitalists, 1861-1901* (New York, 1934)

Josephson, Matthew, *Edison: A Biography* (New York, 1959)

Kirkland, Edward C., *Business in the Gilded Age* (Madison, 1952)

Kirkland, Edward C., *Dream and Thought in the Business Community, 1860-1900* (Ithaca, N.Y., 1956)

Kirkland, Edward C., *Industry Comes of Age: Business, Labor and Public Policy, 1860-1897* (New York, 1961)

Kolko, Gabriel, *Railroads and Regulation, 1877-1916* (Princeton, 1965)

Letwin, William, *Law and Economic Policy in America: The Evolution of the Sherman Anti-Trust Act* (New York, 1965)

Nelson, Daniel, *Frederick W. Taylor and the Rise of Scientific Management* (Madison, Wisc., 1980)

Nevins, Allan, *A Study in Power: John D. Rockefeller, Industrialist and Philanthropist* (2 vols., New York, 1953)

Paul, Arnold M., *Conservative Crisis and the Rule of Law: Attitudes of Bar and Bench, 1887-1895* (Ithaca, N.Y., 1960)

Thorelli, Hans B., *The Federal Anti-Trust Policy* (Baltimore, 1955)

Wall, Joseph F., *Andrew Carnegie* (New York, 1970)

A Machine Era

Ackerman, Carl W., *George Eastman* (Boston and New York, 1930)

Anderson, Oscar E., *Refrigeration in America: A History of a New Technology and its Impact* (Princeton, 1953)

Burlingame, Roger, *Engines of Democracy: Inventions and Society in Mature America* (New York, 1940)

Cooper, Grace R., *The Invention of the Sewing Machine* (Washington, D.C., 1968)

Current, Richard N., *The Typewriter and the Men who made it* (Urbana, Ill., 1954)

Davies, Margery W., *Woman's Place Is at the Typewriter: Office Work and Office Workers, 1870-1930* (Philadelphia, 1982)

Frantz, Joe B. *Gail Borden: Dairyman to a Nation* (Norman, Okla., 1951)

Kaempffert, Waldemar, ed., *A Popular History of American Invention* (2 vols., New York, 1924)

Morison, Elting E., *Men, Machines and Modern Times* (Cambridge, Mass., 1966)

Oliver, John W., *History of American Technology* (New York, 1956)

Steinman, D. B., *The Builders of the Bridge: The Story of John Roebling and his Son* (New York, 1950)

Chapter 2: THE GILDED AGE

Scramble for the Spoils

Barclay, Thomas S., *The Liberal Republican Movement in Missouri, 1865-1871* (Columbia, Mo., 1926)

Callow, Alexander B., *The Tweed Ring* (New York, 1966)

Coleman, Charles H., *The Election of 1868: The Democratic Effort to Regain Control* (New York, 1933)

Fuess, Claude M., *Carl Schurz, Reformer (1829-1906)* (New York, 1932)

Hesseltine, William B., *Ulysses S. Grant, Politician* (New York, 1935)

Hoogenboom, Ari A., *Outlawing the Spoils: The Civil Service Reform Movement 1865-1883* (Urbana, Ill., 1961)

Kehl, James A., *Boss Rule in the Gilded Age: Matt Quay of Pennsylvania* (Pittsburgh, Penn., 1981)

Mandelbaum, Seymour J., *Boss Tweed's New York* (New York, 1965)

Nevins, Allan, *Hamilton Fish: The Inner History of the Grant Administration* (New York, 1936)

Ross, Earl D., *The Liberal Republican Movement* (New York, 1919)

Sproat, John G., *"The Best Men": Liberal Reformers in the Gilded Age* (New York, 1968)

Politics of Stalemate

Barnard, Harry, *Rutherford B. Hayes and His America* (Indianapolis, 1954)

Davison, Kenneth E., *The Presidency of Rutherford B. Hayes* (Westport, Conn., 1972)

Doenecke, Justus D., *The Presidencies of James A. Garfield and Chester A. Arthur* (Lawrence, Kans., 1981)

Faulkner, Harold U., *Politics, Reform and Expansion* (New York, 1959)

Garraty, John A., *The New Commonwealth, 1877-1890* (New York, 1968)

Hollingsworth, J. Rogers, *The Whirligig of Politics: The Democracy of Cleveland to Bryan* (Chicago, 1963)

Marcus, Robert D., *Grand Old Party: Political Structure in the Gilded Age, 1880-1896* (New York, 1971)

Morgan, H. Wayne, *From Hayes to McKinley: National Party Politics* (Syracuse, 1969)

Nevins, Allan, *Grover Cleveland: A Study in Courage* (New York, 1932)

Rothman, David J., *Politics and Power: The United States Senate, 1869-1901* (Cambridge, Mass., 1966)

Sievers, Harry J., *Benjamin Harrison, Hoosier President: The White House and After* (New York, 1968)

Smith, Theodore C., *The Life and Letters of James Abram Garfield* (2 vols., New Haven, 1925)

Chapter 3: THE WORK FORCE

The New Americans

Berthoff, Rowland T., *British Immigrants in Industrial America, 1790-1950* (Cambridge, Mass., 1953)

Brown, Thomas N., *Irish-American Nationalism, 1870-1890* (Philadelphia, 1966)

Erickson, Charlotte, *American Industry and the European Immigrant, 1860-1885* (Cambridge, Mass., 1957)

Handlin, Oscar, *The Uprooted: The Epic Story of the Great Migrations that made the American People* (Boston, 1951)

Higham, John, *Strangers in the Land: Patterns of American Nativism, 1860-1925* (New Brunswick, N.J., 1955)

Howe, Irving, *World of Our Fathers* (New York, 1976)

Kinzer, Donald L., *An Episode in Anti-Catholicism: The American Protective Association* (Seattle, 1964)

Nelli, Humbert S., *Italians in Chicago, 1880-1930: A Study in Ethnic Mobility* (New York, 1967)

Rischin, Moses, *The Promised City: New York's Jews, 1870-1914* (Cambridge, Mass., 1962)

Saloutos, Theodore, *The Greeks in the United States* (Cambridge, Mass., 1964)

Solomon, Barbara M., *Ancestors and Immigrants: A Changing New England Tradition* (Cambridge, Mass., 1956)

Labor on the Move

Avrich, Paul, *The Haymarket Tragedy* (Princeton, N.J., 1984)

Broehl, Wayne G., Jr., *The Molly Maguires* (Cambridge, Mass., 1964)

Bruce, R. V., *1877: Year of Violence* (Indianapolis, 1959)

David, Henry, *The History of the Haymarket Affair* (New York, 1936)

Grob, Gerald N., *Workers and Utopia: A Study of Ideological Conflict in the American Labor Movement, 1865-1900* (Evanston, Ill., 1961)

Gutman, Herbert G., *Work, Culture, and Society in Industrializing America: Essays in American Working-Class and Social History* (New York, 1976)

Herder, Dirk, ed., *American Labor and Immigrant History, 1877-1920s: Recent European Research* (Urbana, Ill., 1983)

Laslett, John, *Labor and the Left: A Study of Socialist and Radical Influences in the American Labor Movement (1881-1924)* (New York, 1970)

McMurray, Donald L., *The Great Burlington Strike of 1888* (Cambridge, Mass., 1956)

Mandel, Bernard, *Samuel Gompers: A Biography* (Yellow Springs, Ohio, 1963)

Powderly, Terence V., *The Path I Trod* (New York, 1940)

Taft, Philip, *The A. F. of L. in the Time of Gompers* (New York, 1957)

Todes, Charlotte, *William H. Sylvis and the National Labor Union* (New York, 1942)

Ware, Norman J., *The Labor Movement in the United States, 1860-1895* (New York, 1929)

Chapter 4: A CULTURE IN TRANSITION

Beer, Thomas, *The Mauve Decade: American Life at the End of the Nineteenth Century* (New York, 1926)

Brooks, Van Wyck, *The Confident Years, 1885-1915* (New York, 1952)

Brooks, Van Wyck, *New England: Indian Summer, 1865-1915* (New York, 1940)

Clark, Clifford E., Jr., *Henry Ward Beecher: Spokesman for a Middle-Class America* (Urbana, Ill., 1978)

Commager, Henry Steele, *The American Mind: An Interpretation of American Thought and Character since the 1880s* (New Haven, 1950)

De Voto, Bernard, *Mark Twain's America* (Boston, 1932)

Ditzion, Sidney H., *Arsenals of a Democratic Culture: A Social History of the American Public Library Movement in New England and the Middle States from 1850 to 1900* (Chicago, 1947)

Feinstein, Howard M., *Becoming William James* (Ithaca, N.Y., 1984)

Fellman, Anita Claire & Michael, *Making Sense of Self: Medical Advice Literature in Late Nineteenth-Century America* (Philadelphia, 1981)

Flexner, James T., *That Wilder Image: The Painting of America's Native School from Thomas Cole to Winslow Homer* (Boston, 1962)

Fox, Daniel M., *Engines of Culture: Philanthropy and Art Museums* (Madison, Wis., 1963)

Hofstadter, Richard, *Social Darwinism in American Thought, 1860-1915* (Philadelphia, 1945)

Johns, Elizabeth, *Thomas Eakins: The Heroism of Modern Life* (Princeton, N.J., 1984)

Kuklick, Bruce, *The Rise of American Philosophy: Cambridge, Massachusetts, 1860-1930* (New Haven, Conn., 1977)

Martin, Jay C., *Harvests of Change: American Literature, 1865-1914* (New York, 1967)

McCullough, David, *Mornings on Horseback* (New York, 1981)

Mumford, Lewis, *The Brown Decades: The Arts in America, 1865-1895* (2nd edn., New York, 1955)

Trachtenberg, Alan, *The Incorporation of America: Culture and Society in the Gilded Age* (New York, 1982)

Vorpahl, Ben M., *Frederic Remington and the West: With the Eye of the Mind* (Austin, Tex., 1978)

Ziff, Larzer, *The American 1890's: Life and Times of a Lost Generation* (London, 1967)

Chapter 5: THE IMPACT OF CHANGE

The Bright Lights of the City

Abell, Aaron I., *The Urban Impact on American Protestantism, 1865-1900* (Cambridge, Mass., 1943)

Boyer, Paul, *Urban Masses and Moral Order in America, 1820-1920* (Cambridge, Mass., 1978)

Dulles, Foster R., *America Learns to Play* (New York, 1940)

Findlay, James F., Jr., *Dwight L. Moody: American Evangelist, 1837-1899* (Chicago, 1969)

Gilbert, Douglas, *American Vaudeville* (New York, 1940)

Green, Constance M., *The Rise of Urban America* (New York, 1965)

Juergens, George, *Joseph Pulitzer and the New York World* (Princeton, 1966)

Lane, James B., *Jacob A. Riis and the American City* (Port Washington, N.Y., 1974)

McKelvey, Blake, *The Urbanization of America, 1860-1915* (New Brunswick, N.J., 1963)

MacLeod, David I., *Building Character in the American Boy: The Boy Scouts, YMCA, and Their Forerunners, 1870-1920* (Madison, Wisc., 1983)

May, Henry F., *The Protestant Churches and Industrial America* (New York, 1949)

Mott, F. L., *A History of American Magazines* (vol. 3, 1865-1885; vol. 4, 1885-1905, New York, 1938, 1957)

Patton, Clifford W., *The Battle for Municipal Reform: Mobilization and Attack, 1875-1900* (Washington, D.C., 1940)

Peel, Robert, *Mary Baker Eddy: The Years of Discovery* (New York, 1966)

Schlesinger, Arthur M., *The Rise of the City, 1878-1898* (New York, 1933)

Swanberg, W.A., *Citizen Hearst* (New York, 1961)

Wealth against Commonwealth

Barker, Charles A., *Henry George* (New York, 1955)

Buck, Solon J., *The Agrarian Crusade* (New Haven, 1920)

Coletta, Paolo E., *William Jennings Bryan, vol. 1. Political Evangelist, 1860-1908* (Lincoln, Neb., 1964)

Destler, Chester M., *Henry Demarest Lloyd and the Empire of Reform* (Philadelphia, 1963)

Durden, Robert F., *The Climax of Populism: The Election of 1896* (Lexington, Ky., 1965)

Glad, Paul W., *McKinley, Bryan and the People* (Philadelphia, 1964)

Goodwyn, Lawrence, *Democratic Promise: The Populist Movement in America* (New York, 1976)

Hicks, John D., *The Populist Revolt* (Minneapolis, 1931)

Kirwan, Albert D., *The Revolt of the Rednecks: Mississippi Politics, 1876-1925* (Lexington, Ky., 1951)

Lindsey, Almont, *The Pullman Strike* (Chicago, 1942)

Palmer, Bruce, *"Man Over Money": The Southern Populist Critique of American Capitalism* (Chapel Hill, N.C., 1980)

Pollack, Norman, *The Populist Response to Industrial America* (Cambridge, Mass., 1962)

Ridge, Martin, *Ignatius Donnelly: The Portrait of a Politician* (Chicago, 1962)

Salvatore, Nick, *Eugene V. Debs: Citizen and Socialist* (Urbana, Ill., 1982)

Shannon, Fred A., *The Farmer's Last Frontier: Agriculture, 1860-1897* (New York, 1945)

Simkins, Francis B., *Pitchfork Ben Tillman, South Carolinian* (Baton Rouge, 1944)

Thomas, John L., *Alternative America: Henry George, Edward Bellamy, Henry Demarest Lloyd, and the Adversary Tradition* (Cambridge, Mass., 1983)

Woodward, C. Vann, *Tom Watson: Agrarian Rebel* (New York, 1938)